The Craftsmanship of Writing

# The Craftsmanship of Writing

Frederic Taber Cooper

WAKING LION PRESS

ISBN 978-1-4341-0309-3

Published by Waking Lion Press, an imprint of The Editorium

The Editorium, LLC
West Valley City, UT 84128-3917
wakinglionpress.com
wakinglion@editorium.com

# Contents

# Preface

The present volume is the outgrowth of a course in essay writing, offered in connection with the University Extension work of Columbia University. It embodies in part what the author then undertook to teach his students, supplemented by what the students quite unconsciously taught the author. There was a class which, taken collectively, offered much diversity of scholarship, a wide range of preparation for writing. Yet one and all of them presented practically the same sort of problem; one and all said in effect: "I have had such and such training; I have worked hard and willingly; yet my manuscripts do not sell. What is the matter with my preparation? What books should I read? What course should I take?" And in a wider way, these are the questions that are today being asked throughout the length and breadth of this continent. Now the purpose of this volume is to answer these questions, by pointing out that the fault is primarily with the would-be authors themselves, and not with their preparation. The best teaching they can anywhere receive is at most a makeshift, a mere starting point; they must learn to rely upon themselves, and the earlier the better. The most that this book or any other can do is to guide them away from certain wrong paths and toward certain right ones; they must cultivate self-criticism, industry, the art of taking infinite pains, the habit of looking upon today's failures as the stepping-stones toward tomorrow's success. The laurels of authorship are worth the winning largely because there is no primrose path leading to them.

Chapter 1

# The Inborn Talent

It is always helpful, in writings possessing even the mildest of text-book flavour, for author and reader to start with a clear mutual understanding of scope and purpose. The best way in which to forestall that aggrieved sense which a student often feels of having derived no profit from a certain book or article or lecture course is to say frankly, at the outset: "Here, in brief, is what we intend to do. If your individual case falls outside these limits, you will waste your time, since it belongs upon the list of what we have no intention of doing."

In the present volume of papers on *The Craftsmanship of Writing,* the best and quickest way to reach this helpful understanding is to explain what first suggested them, and what results it is hoped that they will achieve. There has probably never been a time when so large a number of men and women, of all sorts and conditions, have yielded to the lure of authorship—and the elemental, naïve and random questions that they often ask shows that there has never been a time when so many were in need of a word of friendly guidance. And this is precisely what the present volume claims to give. It does not pretend to point a royal road to literature—to furnish a new philosopher's stone for transmuting ordinary citizens into famous poets and novelists. It has no ambition to create new authors—since authors worthy of the name are born, not made—nor to compete with the efforts of our college English Departments, our summer lecture courses, our correspondence schools and literary agencies—for we have a surfeit of these already. The aim of *The Craftsmanship of*

*Writing* is nothing more pretentious than to help would-be writers to reach a somewhat saner, more logical understanding of the real nature of the profession they are entering upon, both on its technical and its artistic side; to discount its delays and disappointments; and above all, to learn to help themselves by intelligent self-criticism. For it is a somewhat curious fact that there is no other line of intellectual work in which a man or a woman may remain, through months and years, so fundamentally ignorant of his or her real worth.

Now the reason why a struggling author may waste years of misdirected effort, without knowing just how good or bad his productions really are, is not difficult to explain. The sources of any workman's knowledge of his worth are practically only three in number: the market value of his ware; his own self-criticism, and the opinions of others. Now it is a common experience among young authors to find through weary months that their wares apparently have no market value at all—this does away with the first source of knowledge. Secondly, the ability to criticise one's self in a detached, impartial way is one of the rarest of human faculties—and not a bit less rare in authors than in other people. Yet, unfortunately, it is upon his own judgment that every young writer must very largely depend. For there is probably no other craft or employment in which it is so difficult to obtain a really authoritative opinion—for the excellent reason that in no other craft or employment is there such a lack of any general requirement, any standard of apprenticeship. Indeed, it is often as hard to guess the potential powers of a beginner in letters as to predict how a raw recruit is likely to conduct himself under fire. Let us, therefore, take up separately these two questions: First, the various kinds of critical opinion a young author is able to obtain upon his writings; secondly, the nature and degree of systematic training it is possible for him to acquire.

But first let us ask one more preliminary detail: where does the raw recruit in the army of authorship mainly come from? In other trades and professions there is some sort of selective barrier: a college degree, a regent's certificate, a Civil Service examination, a Union Membership, some sort of initial guarantee of fitness. Then, too, in many cases, there is the prohibitive question of expense. It costs both time and money to become a lawyer or physician—even to go upon the stage means nowadays a year or two in a dramatic school, if one does not want to start with a handicap. In contrast writing seems so simple; pen and ink, a pad of paper, a table in a quiet corner—these to the uninitiated seem to be the net amount of required capital. Frank Norris, in a burst of rather curious optimism, once wrote, "The would-be novel writer may determine between breakfast and dinner to essay the plunge, buy (for a few cents) ink and paper between dinner and supper, and have the novel under way before bedtime. How much of an outlay does his first marketable novel represent? Practically nothing." Mr. Norris seems for the moment to have forgotten that his own first "marketable novel," *McTeague* (although published subsequently to *Moran of the Lady Letty*), represented careful labour scattered over a period of four years, and that a portion of it at least necessitated quite literally a further delay than that of ink and paper, being submitted in part fulfillment of the requirements of a course at Harvard University. La Bruyere came considerably nearer the truth when he cynically wrote, from a different angle:

> A man starts upon a sudden, takes Pen, Ink and Paper, and without ever having had a thought of it before, resolves within himself to write a Book; he has no Talent at writing, but he wants fifty Guineas.

Now, as in every other attempt to obtain a high rate of interest upon a small investment, the results are extremely precarious. The difference in this particular case of the beginner in literature is that the fault lies less with the investment than with the investor. Out of a hundred beginners, taken at random, no two have had the same sort or degree of training, the same advantages of worldly knowledge, the same allotment of that special fitness which it is convenient to speak of as the Inborn Talent. And it would be most extraordinary if all of them, or any considerable portion of them should have. The field is open to all corners, without prejudice of colour, sex or age. And so we find competing side by side, the university man, with half a dozen letters after his name; the young woman from some Western farm, who thinks herself a second Mrs. Browning; the underpaid teacher, the starveling minister, the physician with a dwindling practice, who seek to eke out a meagre income with an occasional magazine article; the society woman and the man of leisure whose whim it is to see themselves in print; the suffragette, the sweet girl graduate, the whole motley host that, rightly or wrongly, believe themselves to have the Inborn Talent. Now, if these new writers seek advice—and sooner or later they practically all of them do—from whom can they seek it? What avenues are open to them?

Some writers, of course, are more fortunately placed than others, in this respect; but in practice it will be found that the usual sources of criticism, whether favourable or hostile, narrow down to four: (1) The biased opinions of interested friends; (2) the bought opinions of professional advisers; (3) the rejections or acceptances of editors, either with or without comment; (4) the published criticisms in the review departments of newspapers and magazines. Now, as already said, there is a certain degree of luck in all four of these sources of criticism. Thus, to take them up in order, the opinions of the first class may not always be biased. A young author may have the good luck to number among his friends or relatives one or more authors of big accomplishment and fine discernment who may serve the place of literary godfather, and who in rare and wonderful instances, such as that of Flaubert and Maupassant, actualise that ideal form of apprenticeship which all the arts enjoy save only that of letters. Again, it sometimes happens that a beginner is fortunate enough to choose for his adviser a professional reader whose horizon happens to be wider than that of the mere market value of literary ware, and whose suggestions stimulate the growth of his mentality as well as of his bank account. And then again, there are editors, who, in spite of the burden they carry, are not always too busy to send, with a rejected manuscript, a line or two of welcome advice to a young author whom they see to be stumbling needlessly—or a few words of equally valued praise to the beginner whose first work shows, through all its crudeness, the unmistakable gleam of the Inborn Talent. And as to the fourth class, that of the professional critic, there are a good many successful authors who freely admit the debt they owe to him for many a frank word of praise or censure in earlier years. Indeed, this last source of outside help ought to be the most disinterested and the most useful of them all. That it is not, is due to two simple and rather obvious facts: first, that it cannot possibly reach the novice in letters until he begins to get his writings into print; secondly, that the rank and file of reviewers think it their duty to speak to the readers of books rather than to the writers of them—to tell the general public why they ought to like or dislike a certain volume, instead of telling the author in what particulars his work was good and in what others it might have been better.

"I believe," says Sir Walter Besant, in his *Autobiography,* "that one can count on ten fingers the few critics whose judgments are lessons of instruction to writers as well as readers."

It is this dearth of real enlightenment that makes so many first attempts—whether poetry or prose, essays, stories or special articles—sheer guess-work, gropings in the dark. Hundreds of first manuscripts, and second and third manuscripts, too, are written with tremulous hopes and fears, absurdly overvalued one moment and blackly despaired of the next. They start out on their travels, meekly submitted "at your usual rates," and soon come homing back, with only the empty civility of a printed slip to save them from the waste-paper basket. That is a fair statement of the average beginner's experience, is it not? And it is looked upon as quite in the natural course of things, a special application of the economic law of supply and demand. It places the young author in the same category with every other class of workman who goes around peddling the produce of his handiwork. And if that produce does not happen to be wanted, there is no logical reason why anyone should be required to buy it, whether it be a sonnet or a sugared waffle.

In an essay entitled *L'Argent dans la Littérature,* Zola writes, with customary bluntness: "The State owes nothing to young writers; the mere fact of having written a few pages does not entitle them to pose as martyrs, because no one will print their work. A shoemaker who has made his first pair of shoes does not force the government to sell them for him. It is the workman's place to dispose of his work to the public. And if he can't do it, if he is a nobody, he remains unknown through his own fault, and quite justly so."

Now it does no good to argue that there is something radically wrong about the present system. It is quite sufficient if we frankly recognise that literature occupies an anomalous position, and to seek for the reason. The great advantage that the arts and professions enjoy in theory over trade and business is that they aim to produce objects of such beauty or service of such importance that the ordinary laws of market value do not apply to them. Aside from literature, there is no profession, excepting the closely allied one of the magazine illustrator, which is subjected to a like degree of precarious uncertainty. Architects, it is true, do occasionally enter plans in a competition for some big public building—but this is an exception to the custom of their craft, a gamble which they enter into voluntarily, fully prepared to be cheerful losers. Young artists may repeatedly have their pictures refused admission to the annual Salons; but at least they have the comfort of knowing that there was just one ground for such refusals, namely, that the pictures were not sufficiently good art. A doctor has some trouble in getting his first case, a lawyer in getting his first brief; but when once they have secured respectively a client and a patient, they count upon being regularly employed; it is inconceivable that they should be dismissed with a printed notice that their dismissal "does not imply a criticism of their intrinsic merits." Even your corner grocer, if you leave him without specified reason and go to a competitor halfway down the block, considers it a criticism, and one that he has a right to resent.

As already implied, there is a very simple reason why the man of letters stands in a class apart. The artist and sculptor, the lawyer and doctor, even the grocer and the plumber, have all in their several ways served a long and relatively costly apprenticeship. They have, to put it colloquially, learned their job before they have been allowed to practise for themselves. Whether they will become distinguished in their several callings or even demonstrate an average skill remains to be proved. But they start with a certain guaranteed fund of foundation knowledge, a certain preliminary craftsmanship. It is conceivable, of course, that a medical student might in his first year, successfully treat some simple case of croup or whooping-cough. But that one achievement would not give him sufficient self-assurance to hang out his sign, even if the laws of his State permitted such recklessness. Yet when the merest tyro in writing happens by some lucky hit to write a story good enough to win acceptance, or even, let us say, a story that has somehow won acceptance although not good enough, his pendulum of self-criticism swings to the outmost verge of elation. He refuses to entertain the possibility of further rejections. He begins to multiply the number of stories he can write a month by the number of months in the year, and the product again by the number of dollars on his first cheque.

Of course, in a majority of cases, such dreams are doomed to the same fate as in the fable of the "Pot of Milk"—and it is fortunate for the world at large, and doubly fortunate for the young author that this is so. The truth is that in literature, as in every other art, there is no such thing as a royal road to fame. Just because a writer is free to hang out his shingle, so to speak, at the very beginning, it does not by any means follow that he is permanently exempted from serving an apprenticeship. And this fact is the sole excuse for dwelling at length upon so cornmonplace a grievance as rejected manuscripts. Every young writer knows, of course, that he faces repeated rejection; but very few recognise that each manuscript that comes back is part of their education, a definite amount of the time and effort which every apprentice is expected to pay.

The present writer well remembers his own first attempts to write short stories, while still a college undergraduate, and his surprise and resentment when one by one the magazines failed to appreciate them. He grudged the labour spent upon them; he felt, in a vague sort of way, that he had been defrauded. College themes, curiously enough, rested on a different basis. The time spent on them involved no irritation, although they were doomed in advance to be still-born. The reason for this difference was that the writer recognised his college themes as part of the cost of preparation, and that he had not yet learned that his rejected manuscripts were also part of that same preparation—and by far the more important part.

"The worst of all evils, for a beginner," says Zola, in the above-mentioned essay, "is to arrive and to succeed too soon. He ought to know that behind every solid reputation there lie at least twenty years of effort and of labour."

What each man or woman learns from a rejection depends, of course, upon the circumstances of the individual case. It may teach nothing more than the unwisdom of submitting a certain type of story or article to one particular magazine; or again, it may bring a salutary awakening to the fact that what the author fondly believed to be a masterpiece is, after all, a rather tawdry and banal performance. But in any case, a setback is wholesome discipline if it makes a writer ask himself seriously what is the matter with his work—for it is better to tear up half a dozen good manuscripts than to let a single bad one find its way into print. "As remediless as bad work once put forward," is a wise little simile of Mr. Kipling's—you will find it in *The Light that Failed,* not far from the point at which the two versions of that story part company. It must, however, be borne in mind that no sort of apprenticeship ever created genius—its utmost value is to develop technical skill. In every art there are two indispensable qualities—an Inborn Talent and a slowly and painfully acquired technique—the only difference, in the case of literature, being that the technique must in the main be self-taught. The Inborn Talent is, by its very definition, a thing unteachable, although it may be discovered, fostered and developed. It can no more be created by teachers of rhetoric or grammar than a singing-master can create a voice. But the would-be singer has this big advantage over the would-be writer, in that he can easily find a teacher of authority who will tell him in the course of a single interview frankly and conclusively whether his case is hopeless or not while the young author has no chance of getting such an opinion, and if he had would probably refuse to credit it.

The result is that most new writers are left to learn their value, slowly and painfully, in the unsparing school of experience. And the nature of the lesson is best grasped by applying it to the analogous art of painting. Suppose the young artist left quite to himself, thrown wholly on his own judgment, regarding subject and composition, colour, light and shade. He paints and paints, picture after picture, with only his instinct to tell him whether they are good or bad—and every now and then someone having authority comes along and blots them out with turpentine or a palette knife, and with no word of explanation. The young artist tries again, and still again—and if he has the Inborn Talent, it is conceivable that he may grow slowly through his own efforts, helped only by this purely destructive criticism, until he achieves real greatness. As a matter of fact, this is not the road over which the great painters have travelled, but it is the road by which the masters of literature have attained their goal.

Now let us suppose, for the sake of argument, that a young writer is in no haste to see himself in print, that he would be glad to have some sort of systematic instruction through a period of years, analogous to that of the other arts and crafts: what possible avenues are open to him? The Inborn Talent, of course, cannot be taught; but the technique of good writing not only can be taught, but ought to be. Yet at present, and I say this advisedly, we have not a single well equipped school of instruction in technique—nothing which even pretends to do for writing what the conservatories do for vocal and instrumental music, and schools like the Beaux Arts for painting and architecture. The odd thing is that people have fallen into the habit of thinking that we do possess such opportunities for instruction. Our schools and colleges and universities are paying more attention than ever to rhetoric and theme writing. Children daily puzzle their parents with intricacies of sentence diagrams and strange nomenclature of grammar undreamed of in an earlier generation. And yet the average city editor will tell you that the young college graduate has almost as much to unlearn as to learn before he becomes a useful member of the staff. The late David Graham Phillips, who heartily concurred in this view of the value of college English, was fond of telling the story of how and why he lost his first newspaper position. It was when he was fresh from his studies at Princeton, that after a good deal of persistence he obtained a position on a leading western newspaper, to which he offered his services free of salary. Although it was mid-winter and the city room was barn-like in temperature, he tells how he used to sit at his desk with the perspiration of mental labour pouring from his brow, while he struggled to make literature with a capital L from such material as "This afternoon John Smith, a house-painter, fell off a ladder and broke his arm." Mr. Phillips had held his unsalaried position for about ten days when the higher power who presided over the paper's destinies happened to come through the city room. "Who is that man?" he asked, indicating Mr. Phillips. The city editor explained. "Discharge him," came the curt mandate. "But we are getting him for nothing," protested the city editor. "I don't care if he is paying for the privilege," came the rejoinder; "discharge him immediately! I can't bear to see any human being work so hard!"

The trouble is that in writing we have confused the medium with the art; we have been content, a good deal of the time, to teach language where we meant to teach technique. Writing differs from the other arts in this: that from earliest childhood, its medium of expression has been more or less familiar, more or less skilfully employed. A child of five who cannot put together simple sentences that express his physical needs is considered mentally deficient; whereas, if he can already whistle or sing a popular air correctly his family indicate the fact with pride; and if he can draw a cow that really looks like a cow and not like an abnormal table endowed with horns and tail, he is an infant prodigy. But if we could conceive of a race of intelligent deaf-mutes whose customary mode of communication was a highly developed picture language, then we might imagine a manual skill of draughtsmanship acquired from early childhood that would place the medium of the painter on an equality with that of the writer today.

Now in our schools and colleges, with the best intentions in the world, what is actually achieved goes very little beyond an increased dexterity in the use of the medium, language. Grammar and rhetoric, even the ability to say quite accurately certain simple and obvious things, do not make up the technique of good writing, any more than the ability to draw a circle or a straight line or to match colours makes up the technique of good painting. And even those few courses which the English departments of our larger universities have in recent years established for the benefit of their graduate students—courses in the structure of the short story and the play and the novel—although they are an encouraging step in the right direction, are not either in kind or in degree quite comparable to the practical training that is open to students in every other branch of art. The best instruction in any craft or profession is a practical training by someone who has already proved himself a master of it. The instructors in our medical schools, our seminaries, our schools of law, are nearly always men who have won their reputation in the sick chamber, the pulpit, the courtroom. And this is the one logical source of learning. Yet in authorship the chance of working directly under the guidance of a master has, so far as I can recall, been exemplified in practice on a large scale only once in the history of letters—and that was in the special brand of historical romance tirelessly produced by the author of *Les Trois Mousquetaires* and his apprentices—satirically designated as *Dumas et Cie, Fabrique de Romans.* College instruction in the art of writing is, with a few brilliant exceptions, given by men who are trained critics rather than creative writers—men who know infinitely more about taking a work to pieces than about putting it together. Dissecting is an important part of class work in a course in botany, but it does not help us to a knowledge of how to grow a rose. And you will learn more about building a cathedral by watching it go together, stone by stone, than by seeing a gang of professional wreckers dustily pulling it down.

Are we to understand, then, someone will ask, that the English courses in colleges and graduate schools are a waste of time? Emphatically no, not by any means, so long as we do not mistake the nature of their help. So far as they go they are of distinct value to a student with ambition for authorship—valuable in the same way that courses in literature and foreign languages are valuable; but they carry him no further in his technical training than college courses in biology or constitutional history carry a student forward in the practice of medicine or the law.

Professor A. S. Hill, whose English courses are a pleasant memory to Harvard men of the older generation, wrote pessimistically only a few years ago, in a little volume entitled *Our English:*

> Under the most favourable conditions, the results of English composition as practiced in college are, it must be confessed, discouraging. The shadow of generations of perfunctory writers seems to rest upon the paper, and only here and there is it broken by a ray of light from the present. . . . I know of no language—ancient or modern, civilized or savage—so insufficient for the purposes of language, so dreary and inexpressive, as theme-language in the mass.

The practical question, then, is: In the absence of special training-schools what advice should be given to a beginner? Are there any lines of special study that he may follow, any form of self-training that he may put himself through? The answer is: Yes, there is the theoretical help of text-books on technique, and there is the practical training of journalism. But it is well to remember, on the one hand, that all the text-books ever written on the English novel will not make a novelist, any more than Ruskin's *Modern Painters,* even though committed to memory, would make a Millais or a Bouguereau.

A newspaper training is a good, wholesome tonic, especially as an antidote to the stilted heaviness of the academic style. It gives a certain fluency, a certain colloquial tone that makes for freedom. "To the wholesome training of severe newspaper work when I was a very young man, I constantly refer my first successes," was Dickens's stereotyped reply to the questions of American reporters.[1] And yet one hesitates to recommend it with the same assurance with which it was to be recommended a quarter century ago. For if the younger generation of American writers have any one conspicuous fault in common, it is that of too journalistic a style.

But there is one question which every amateur writer should ask himself in advance of everything else, and that is: Has he the Inborn Talent? Has he any talent at all, anything worth the saying—worth, that is, the trouble of learning to say in the best possible manner? Has he ideas?—not mere raw material, in the form of things seen and experiences lived but ideas about them that may be of importance or interest to some portion of the world at large. Let us ask this direct question of every man and woman who reads these pages: Have you taken any pains to satisfy yourself that you possess this Inborn Talent? If not, do so without delay, before you scatter futile ink over another sheet of wasted paper. And it is not just a question of having or not having the creative instinct, but of having it in sufficient degree to make its development really worth while. For the Inborn Talent in a writer may be compared to the grade of ore

---

1. The late Edouard Rod declared himself even more emphatically in favour of a newspaper training: "Journalism is an excellent school: it stimulates sluggish minds, it disciplines roving imaginations, it brings into direct contact with the public certain writers who otherwise would have remained unknown to the general public, and who during the process of becoming known, learn reciprocally to know their public. This is useful and healthy: because it is, after all, for others that we write. . . . The school of journalism is exacting and wearisome, it is true; but that is not an evil. Certain writers, they tell you, in the slang of the editorial room, 'write themselves dry;' but it is only those who had nothing of importance to lose."

in a mine—the question is not simply whether there is any precious metal there at all, but whether it is present in paying quantities. It is well to find out, if you can, just how richly your talent will assay, and then work it accordingly.

But, you may retort, how is any one to find out whether he has talent? Who is to be the judge? I-low can the author himself or any one else know surely whether repeated rejections through a course of months mean hopeless mediocrity or the handicap of crude methods—whether improvement is a matter of being born again or merely of buckling down and laboriously learning the job? And just here, of course, lies the real difficulty of making this advice practical. No one can answer this first and most important question for you—no one, at least, so authoritatively as to convince you even against your will. But you yourself can answer a few frank questions that will go a long way toward enlightening you: Why are you trying to write? What preparations have you had that make you believe you are qualified? How long ago did you begin to try? What sort of encouragement have you so far received? These are questions which no one else can answer for you; for no two cases are precisely alike. But you cannot answer them honestly without having a strong conviction steal over you either that you have or that you have not the Inborn Talent.

Do you write, for instance, as the born artist paints or the born musician plays, because you feel a compelling necessity for self-expression? Or do you write as the house painter wields his brush or the barrel-organ man turns his handle, merely for the sake of the dollars or the dimes? Have you strong prejudices in regard to the kind of writing you are ready to do? Or are you willing to write in any form, on any subject, from a sonnet to a breakfast food advertisement? Most of us at one time or another have found ourselves under the temporary necessity of doing something more or less in the nature of "hack-work," work that not only meant drudgery but that took us away from bigger, finer things. Yet it is not the willingness to do "hack-work" and to do it cheerfully and thoroughly, when the occasion demands, that proves we lack the Inborn Talent—it is the failure to distinguish between what is "hack-work" and what is not; the spirit of indifference which looks upon all kinds of writing indiscriminately as a marketable produce, that degrades authorship from a profession to a trade.

Or again, what has been your preparation, up to the time when you send off your first essay or poem or story, stamps enclosed, to take its chances with some editor? Does your real apprenticeship begin now with its toll of disappointments and delays; manuscripts that grow soiled and shabby and one by one are consigned to the waste-basket? Or have you been unconsciously apprenticed to litera-ture from early childhood, surrounded by an atmosphere of books, absorbing, because you could not help it, correct ideas of form and technique from the daily conversation around you? Are you still in the first enthusiasm of youth with your views of life still mainly rose-coloured dreams? Or have you spent the first thirty or forty years of your life face to face with hard realities, in the activities of business or of travel and adventure—as a soldier of fortune rather than man of letters? It does not follow that in the one case you haves the inborn literary instinct and that in the other you have not. Ruskin at the age of five had already entered upon his apprenticeship. Before he had learned to write, he had taught himself a makeshift method of vertical printing with a pencil, and had undertaken a story in three-volume form, the name of which escapes the memory, and really does not matter. The significant thing about it is that this precocious child of five was already so saturated with the atmosphere of books, so familiar with their form and make-up, that with the imitative fidelity of his age, he added to his own work a carefully compiled page of *errata*. Sir Walter Besant, after having endured a six years' exile, occupying a Colonial Professorship on the island of Mauritius, records upon his return, "I began life again at the age of thirty-one; my capital was a pretty extensive knowledge acquired by voracious and indiscriminate reading."

Mr. Morgan Robertson, the writer of sea stories, is a conspicuous example of a man who for years had lived apart from books, one decade before the mast, and another as an expert diamond setter and then suddenly surprised himself by revealing the Inborn Talent. But his is an exceptional case. There are a good many men whose love of adventure has given them a rich variety of experience, whose early life has been spent in the danger-places of the world. They are apt to think that they possess the gift because they have the material—and yet these two things have practically nothing in common. It is not the material but the instinct to use it in the right way that makes the Inborn Talent. It is quite a common experience to have men come for advice who have spent years in queer, out-of-the-way corners of the earth and have had adventures rich in thrills and shudders, such as would make *Robinson Crusoe* or *Treasure Island* sound a little tame; and almost invariably what they say is this: "We have the material. Teach us the technique!" Yet in the majority of cases even a knowledge of technique would probably not make stories that they would write sound otherwise than commonplace. For it is one of the commonest things in the world to find that men can live adventurous lives without being really aware of it in a big dramatic sense—that they can pass through places of great danger, inimitable strangeness, matchless beauty; and yet when they come to write them down, they might just as well be describing adventures in their own back yard.

The Inborn Talent, then, is something distinct from the material of our experience and the technical use we make of that material. Just what it is proves rather baffling to define. But at least it includes several different elements: First, the art of really seeing—the artist's eye, which looks through and beyond the mere outward material aspect and sees the vision of some great, unpainted picture. Secondly, a fine instinct for the value of words—a gift that is something quite different from mere richness of vocabulary on the one hand, and the possession of style, on the other. Vocabulary may be increased at will by patiently memorising a dictionary; and style is a matter of cadence and sound sequence—it is quite possible to write rather sad trash in an impeccable style. But a sense of the value of words, an instinct for finding, within the limits of our spoken language, the precise word and phrase that will as nearly as possible convey a thought that is perhaps bigger or subtler than any spoken words—this indeed stamps the possessor as having the Inborn Talent. And lastly, it includes the possession of ideas, as distinct from knowledge. You may know a vast number of useful facts, such as that a straight line is the shortest dis-tance between two points—but such knowledge no more constitutes the Inborn Talent than such a definition constitutes literature. But ideas, big, vital ideas, of the compelling sort that force themselves into written words, in the face of obstacles and disappointments and the inertia of public indifference, are the very essence of the creative spirit, the golden hallmark of the Inborn Talent.

Chapter 2

# The Power of Self-Criticism

Let us assume, from this point onward, that any would-be writer whose eye happens to fall upon these pages possesses in some degree that quality which is inborn and not made—the potential force of authorship. The next all-important question is, how is this inborn talent to be best developed? What is the first faculty for a young author to cultivate? The answer may be given with emphatic assurance: The faculty of self-criticism. Yet a good many teachers will answer differently; they will tell you that in writing, as in everything else that is worth doing well, the one indispensable factor is perseverance, industry, the tenacity that sticks to a task until that task is mastered. In a certain sense the teachers who say this are right. There is just one way of learning to do a thing, and that is by doing it—doing it over and over, until the trick of it is mastered—and this holds just as true of the trick of constructing a short story as of that of kneading bread. But all the industry in the world will not take you far if it is misdirected. No amount of wasted flour and wasted energy will make a baker of you, if you cannot tell good bread from bad—and no amount of straining thought and patient twisting and untwisting of the threads of a plot will make a good short story if you do not know the right twist from the wrong.

For this reason, a young author who has developed the power of self-criticism enjoys a distinct advantage. He has within him the ability to help himself as no one else can help him. Others may tell him whether his work is good or bad; but only the author himself is in a position to know just what he was trying to do and how far short he has fallen of doing it. It is easy for a critic of broad sympathies and keen discernment to point out a writer's faults and to show how a specific piece of bad writing may be worked over and improved. But in a big, general way it may be said boldly that no one can teach a writer how to remedy his faults, no one can provide a golden rule for his future avoidance of them. Suppose, for instance, that an author's trouble is in plot construction. It may be easy to tell him where his plot is wrong and explain to him the principle that he has violated. But if he is to obtain any real and lasting profit he must find out for himself how to set the trouble right. Of course, you might construct the plot for him—but then it would be your plot and not his; you would be, not his teacher, but his collaborator; and his working out of your plot would almost surely result in bad work. Or suppose again that his fault is one of style. You may point out that his prose lacks rhythm, that his language is pompous, or high-coloured, or vulgar. You may remedy specific paragraphs with a rigorous blue pencil; but the writer must learn for himself how to acquire an ear for rhythm or a sense of good taste in word and phrase.

Unfortunately the power to judge one's own work with the detachment and impartiality of an outsider is so rare a quality that we may seriously question whether any author ever acquires it in an absolute sense. Many writers of distinction have been to the end of their lives notoriously unable to discriminate between their good work and their bad. Wordsworth is a flagrant case in point.[1] Mark Twain, in our own generation, is another—or else the genius that produced *Tom Sawyer* and *Innocents Abroad* would never have allowed such sorry stuff as *Adam's Diary* to don the dignity of print. Other writers, even some of the greatest, can get the proper outside perspective of their work only by some systematic method, some mechanical device. Balzac, for instance, needed the impersonality of the printed page before he could judge the value of his writings or do any effective

---

1. Walter Pater, in *Appreciations,* says: "Nowhere is there so perplexed a mixture as in Wordsworth's own poetry, of work touched with intense and individual power, with work of almost no character at all. . . . Of all poets equally great he would gain most by a skilfully made anthology." And similarly Lowell, in his essay entitled "Shakespeare Once More": "His (Wordsworth's) poems are Egyptian sand-wastes, with here and there an oasis of exquisite greenery, a grand image Sphinx-like, half buried in drifting commonplaces, or a solitary pillar of some towering thought."

revision; it was only through repeated sets of proof sheets that much of his work slowly grew into final shape.[1]

Now this vital power of self-criticism, which even great writers have, many of them, developed slowly and painfully, is at best rudimentary in the average beginner. Every writer, whether he will or not, puts a good deal of himself into his work; and every amateur writer is inordinately pleased with that part of his work which he feels to be distinctive, that quality which stamps it as his own. It may bristle with mannerisms, as a hedgehog bristles with spines nevertheless it is the part dearest to him, the part that he is slowest to recognise as wrong. He cannot see himself as others see him. How is this rudimentary sense to be developed? First of all, it would seem, by learning to criticise others. Writing in this respect does not differ from shoeing a horse or making a pair of trousers. If you have not learned to judge whether a horse is well shod or a pair of trousers well cut, then you may go through life without knowing the quality of your own work as blacksmith or tailor. What you must do is to go to blacksmiths and to tailors of recognised skill and patiently study their methods and their results until you make yourself an expert on these subjects—perhaps, even, until you discover ways in which their work may be improved. And the same rule holds good, if instead of horseshoes and trousers you wish to learn the craftsmanship of essay and sonnet.

Now, it is far easier to say, Learn to criticise others, than it is to tell how to go to work to learn. But the first and weightiest rule is this: begin by reading the best models in whatever line of work you are desirous of taking up. Go to the fountain-head, read the books themselves, don't read what someone else has written about them—or if you do, at least make such reading a secondary matter. If your chosen field is the short story, spend your time in reading the recognised masterpieces of Poe and Maupassant, Kipling and O. Henry, in preference to the best text-book ever written on short-story structure. If your life work is lyric poetry, then by all means read lyrics, memorise lyrics, the best you can find and the more the better. You may get some help from critical studies, but you will get vastly

---

1. See page 163.

more from the knowledge which you slowly and laboriously dig out for yourself. When someone once wrote to Matthew Arnold on behalf of a young woman who thought that she possessed the poetic gift and wished to know if there was such a thing as a dictionary of rhymes, he replied: "There is a *Rhyming Dictionary* and there is a book called a *Guide to English Verse Composition.* But all this is sad lumber, and the young lady had much better content herself with imitating the metres she finds most attract her in the poetry she reads. Nobody, I imagine, ever began to good purpose in any other way."

It is rather surprising and extremely suggestive to find how many of the world's great writers were insatiable and omnivorous readers in early youth. Pope records that as a boy "I took to reading by myself, for which I had a very great eagerness and enthusiasm. . . . I followed everywhere as my fancy led me, and was like a boy gathering flowers in the fields and woods just as they fell his way." Moore, in his *Life of Byron,* gives a list which the author of *Childe Harold* jotted down from memory, of books read before he was twenty[1]—a list so varied and extensive as to make many a mature man of letters of his day feel sadly delinquent. George Eliot, at about the same age, writes to a friend as follows: "My mind is an assemblage of disjointed specimens of history, ancient and modern, scraps of poetry picked up from Shakespeare, Cowper, Wordsworth and Milton; newspaper topics; morsels of Addison and Bacon, Latin verbs, geometry, entomology and chemistry; reviews and metaphysics." Theophile Gautier is perhaps, the most extreme instance that can be cited. He learned to read at the age of five. "And since that time," he adds, "I may say, like Apelles, *Nulla dies sine linea.*" And his biographer, Maxime du Camp, says further:

> This is literally true; I do not think there. ever existed a more indefatigable reader than Gautier. Any book was good enough to

---

1. In the list referred to, the books are grouped under the headings, History, Biography, Law, Philosophy, Geography, Poetry, Eloquence, Divinity, and Miscellaneous, concluding with the following paragraph: "All the books here enumerated I have taken down from memory. I recollect reading them and can quote passages from any mentioned. I have, of course, omitted several in my catalogue, but the greater part of the above I perused before the age of fifteen. . . . I have also read (to my regret at present) about four thousand novels, including the works of Cervantes, Fielding, Smollett, Richardson, Mackenzie, Sterne, Rabelais, Rousseau, etc."

satisfy this tyrannical taste, that at times seemed to degenerate into a mania. . . . He took pleasure in the most mediocre novels, equally with books of high philosophic conceptions, and with works of pure science. He was devoured with the thirst for learning, and he used to say, "There is no conception so poor, no trash so detestable, that it does not teach something from which one may profit." He would read dictionaries, grammars, prospectuses, cook-books, almanacs. . . . He had no sort of system about his reading; whatever book came under his hand he would open with a sort of mechanical movement, nor lay it down again until he had turned the closing page.

Now there may be some disadvantages in this sort of voracious and undisciplined reading, in which many a famous author has confessedly indulged. But at least it tends toward forming an independent taste and avoiding the slavish echoing of cut-and-dried academic judgments. In an essay entitled "Is it Possible to Tell a Good Book from a Bad One?" Mr. Augustine Birrell remarks pertinently: "To admire by tradition is a poor thing. Far better really to admire Miss Gabblegoose's novels than to pretend to admire Miss Austen's." There is nothing so deadening to the critical faculty as the blind acceptance of text-book and encyclopedic verdicts. No critical estimate of any author, living or dead, is ever quite final. As Anatole France is fond of reminding us, even Homer, has not been admired for precisely the same reasons during any two consecutive centuries." The works that everyone admires are those that no one examines. We receive them as a precious burden, which we pass on to others without having looked at them." And in much the same vein, Dr. Oliver Wendell Holmes once wrote: "Nothing is interesting to all the world. An author who is spoken of as universally admired will find, if he is foolish enough to inquire, that there are not wanting intelligent persons who are indifferent to him, nor yet those who have a special emphatic dislike to him." Unless you are devoid of literary taste, you must find pleasure in a certain number of the recognised masters; but you are under no obligation to admire them all.[1] The ability to

---

1. This is practically the thought of Thoreau, when he wrote: "If the writers of the brazen age are most suggestive to thee, confine thyself to them and leave those of the Augustan age to dust and the bookworm."

give an intelligent reason for differing from the accepted estimate of Milton, or Fielding, or Dickens, is not a bad test of the possession of the critical gift. "A man," says George Eliot, "who dares to say that he finds an eminent classic feeble here, extravagant there, and in general overrated, may chance to give an opinion which has some genuine discrimination in it concerning a new worker or a living thinker."

As a basis, then, for forming a sound critical estimate of books, one needs: first, a broad acquaintance with the best authors, the wider and more catholic the better; secondly, an open and independent mind. If, beyond this, your taste happens to run to a serious study of criticism, its history, its methods, its controversies, all this will tend to strengthen your self-confidence and sureness of touch. Yet, for the purpose of craftsmanship, the principles on which to judge a book are few and simple. You are not required to dogmatise about the ultimate value, in the universal scheme of things, of the newest novel or the youngest verse. As a craftsman you are interested primarily in its possible present value to you. Accordingly, there is just one way in which to judge the books you read, the new books equally with the old: and that is, to ask yourself what was the author's underlying purpose, what special means he took to accomplish it, and whether or not he attained his goal. The further question, whether the thing was worth doing at all, concerns the craftsman only indirectly just as the question whether a cube and cone and pyramid are worth reproducing in black and white need never trouble the art student. If his purpose is to draw a cube or a cone, then his one concern is to find out how to do it in the best possible way. The moral or ethical value of a painting or a book is not a part of the craftsmanship of art or of literature. The one paramount question is always: What did the author try to do, and how near did he come to doing it? This form of criticism, which seeks to classify books according to the author's purpose, is very nearly what Mr. Howells had in mind when he wrote:

> It is hard for the critic to understand that it is really his business to classify and analyse the fruits of the human mind very much as the naturalist classifies the objects of his study, rather than to praise or blame them; that there is a measure

of the same absurdity in his trampling on a poem, a novel or an essay that does not please him as in a botanist grinding a plant underfoot because he does not find it pretty. He does not conceive that it is his business rather to identify the species, and then explain how and where the species is imperfect and irregular.

It has already been said that the young writer can get comparatively small aid from volumes of criticism and monographs on how to write; that he should go to the authors who have produced literature rather than to those who tell others how to produce it. There is, however, one class of critical essay, the importance of which, to the young writer, can hardly be overrated; and that is the criticism written by men who have proved themselves masters of the art they criticise. I have in mind such essays as that of Poe, in which he analyses the structure of *The Raven;* Maupassant's introduction to *Pierre et Jean;* and Valdes's introduction to *La Hermana San Sulpicio;* Trollope's chapter on the novel in his *Autobiography;* and in general the various critical writings of Zola and Anatole France, Henry James and William Dean Howells the list could be amplified at pleasure in which they allow themselves to theorise freely about their conception of the art they practise and the methods by which they strive to produce their results. Every page of such criticism is in the nature of a craftsman's confessions—they are full of priceless illumination.

Yet it cannot be too strongly insisted that, in writing far more than in painting, there is a great deal that cannot be taught and that you must think out for yourself. One reason, undoubtedly, is that the craftsmanship of letters is more elastic than that of the other arts—there is scope for a greater freedom and originality. Henry James, in *The Art of Fiction,* shrewdly says: "The painter is able to teach the rudiments of his practice, and it is possible, from the study of good work (granted the aptitude) both to learn how to paint and to learn how to write. Yet . . . the literary artist would be obliged to say to his pupil much more than the other, 'Oh, well, you must do it as you can.'" Again, there are some things which an author cannot teach because he does not quite know how or why he did a certain thing. Oftentimes a novelist achieves some of his happiest results unconsciously,[1] and by sheer instinct; and then, again, a carefully planned chapter or in some cases an entire volume fails of its effect, and the reason of the failure eludes him.[2] These are the sort of questions which a young writer should have constantly before him, in all his reading: Why is a certain chapter tedious and a certain other chapter tingling with an almost painful suspense? And did the author mean to achieve these results, or has he simply failed in what he tried to do? Take, for example, two passages from Kipling; not perhaps the best we might find for the purpose, but at least they are to the point—the one conveying the sense of dragging, monotonous hours, the other that of tremendous speed, the conquest of time and space. On the one hand we have in *The Light that Failed* the unforgettable picture of Dick sitting, day after day, in his unending darkness, dumbly turning over Maisie's letters, which he is never to read; on the other, in *Captains Courageous,* we see Harvey Cheyne's father speeding across the breadth of the American continent, goaded by an intolerable impatience to reach the son, whom by a miracle the waves have given back to him. Now, the first case is flawless. The second, much praised and often quoted, is off the key. That private car of the elder Cheyne, "humming like a giant bee" across

---

1. Thackeray, in *Vanity Fair,* writing the chapter describing how Rawdon Crawley, released from the sponging house, returns to his home to find Lord Steyne in Becky's company and hurls the noble blackguard to the ground, gives the final touch with "Becky admired her husband, strong, brave and victorious." After he had written these words the novelist dropped his pen and brought his fist down on the table. "By God! That's a stroke of genius!"

2. Mr. Henry James's own confessions regarding *The Awkward Age,* contained in the preface to the "New York Edition," seems very much to the point: "That I did, positively and seriously—ah, so seriously—emulate the levity of Gyp and by the same token, of that hardiest of flowers fostered in her school, M. Henri Lavedan, is a contribution to the history of *The Awkward Age* that I shall obviously have had to brace myself in order to make. . . . My private inspiration had been in the Gyp plan (artfully dissimulated, for dear life, and applied with the very subtlest consistency, but none the less kept in secret view); yet I was to fail to make out in the event that the book succeeded in producing the impression of *any* plan on any person. No hint of that sort of success, or of any critical perception at all in relation to the business, has ever come my way. . . . I had meanwhile been absent in England, and it was not until my return, some time later, that I had from my publisher any news of our venture. But the news then met at a stroke all my curiosity: am sorry to say the book has done nothing to speak of; I've never in all my experience seen one treated with more general and complete disrespect."

mountain and prairie, by the very sense of motion it conveys, robs us of a true perception of the way in which time seems to drag to the impatient man within it.

But above all, in your reading, do not be content with studying the so-called masterpieces of literature. It is wise to know the *Decameron* and *Don Quixote,* Richardson, and Smollett, and Sterne; but the modern writer can no more depend upon them as models than the modern painter can depend upon Botticelli and Ghirlandajo. A knowledge of Elisabethan footgear, or of the relative artistic value of the moccasin and the *sabot,* is of little value to a modern shoemaker. What he wants to know is how shoes, the best sort of shoes, are made today, by the latest methods. And it is precisely the same with literature. There is no demand today for a new *Hamlet,* a second *Paradise Lost,* another Sir Roger de Coverley, or even a *Tom Jones, David Copperfield* or *Vanity Fair.* The technique of writing is constantly in a state of transition; and however much we may delight in the methods of a generation or a century ago, we do not tolerate them at the hands of modern writers. Take for instance the modern novel; its form and structure—one might almost say its spirit, too—have been radically changed from that of Thackeray and Dickens. And it does not help us nearly so much, as writers, to know which of the two is the greater novelist, as to understand in what respects Henry James and Maupassant are better craftsmen than either of them. Professor Woodberry, in *The Appreciation of Literature,* insists that, even for the general reader, "the serious study of one's own literature is most fruitfully begun by acquaintance with those authors who are in vogue and nearly contemporary." In the case of the would-be writer it is not merely most fruitful, but absolutely imperative, to keep abreast of the best contemporary work that is done in the field of his own labours. And by "best work" I do not mean only such books as seem likely to stand the test of time, books that are unmistakably big in theme, in purpose and in technical skill: contemporary works of this class are so few that the apprentice's lesson would be soon ended. No, I go much further than that and include all the new books which exhibit even in some single direction, an encouraging tendency, the evidence of some problem faced and solved, some interesting innovation attempted. Above all, in your reading, avoid that narrow provincial spirit that limits your range to the works of your own countrymen. The American writer cannot afford to ignore what is being done in his own field by Englishmen. And if he has the time and the gift of languages he will be the broader and better artist for keeping abreast of the best thought and best work of France and Germany and Italy.

And in all your studies let the two great essentials, reading and writing, go hand in hand. Clarify your impressions by transferring them to paper. They may never be of value to anyone else, but they will be of inestimable service to you, as milestones of your own progress. "Of late years," wrote Trollope at the close of his autobiography, "I have found my greatest pleasure in our old English dramatists, not from excessive love of their work, but from curiosity in searching their plots and examining their character. If I live a few years longer, I shall, I think, leave in my copies of these dramatists, down to the close of James I, written criticisms on every play." In Zola's published *Lettres de Jeunesse,* letters written between the ages of twenty and twenty-two, the chief interest centres in their testimony of the eagerness with which he devoured books, the earnestness with which he thought about them, and the enthusiasm with which he poured out his opinions upon paper. Through those rapid, immature and often turgid pages one sees already the germs of ideas that later came to fruition, the origin of many of his articles of literary faith. And not so far removed was the method by which an author of widely different quality and creed learned his craftsmanship. This paragraph from Stevenson's letters, though often quoted, will hurt no one to read once again:

> All through my boyhood and youth I was known and pointed out for the pattern of an idler; and yet I was always busy on my private end, which was to learn to write. I always kept two books in my pocket, one to read, the other to write in. As I walked, my mind was busy fitting what I saw with appropriate words; when I sat by the roadside, I would either read, or a pencil and a penny version-book would be in my hand, to note down the features of the scene or commemorate some halting stanzas. . . . And what I wrote was for no ulterior use; it was

written consciously for practice. . . . I had vowed that I would learn to write. That was a proficiency that tempted me, and I practiced, to acquire it, as a man learns to whittle, in a wager with myself.

But in all your studies of other writers, the living and the dead, cultivate independence. Never slavishly imitate. Take what you find best from the technique of each book you read and reject the rest. Notice what qualities and what defects the authors you read have in common and what are their individual sins and virtues. In learning your lesson from them, do not be afraid of independence, so long as you know the reason why. But as Miss Ellen Terry remarks aptly, in her volume of autobiography, before you are allowed to be eccentric you must have learned where the centre is. Mistrust the extravagant individualism of youth; realise that there is no virtue in being different, unless the difference produces some deliberately sought result. To come down from your apartment by the fire-escape will no doubt make you conspicuous—but there is really no point in doing so unless the elevator has stopped running and the stairs are on fire. In writing we want some better and more logical reason for eccentricity than a mere peacock vanity, a desire to attract attention. Where a literary form is well established, do your share in maintaining it, excepting when you have some excellent reason for making a change. The chances are that in doing a thing differently from the established formula you will not do it half so well. Only a madman would try to write a sonnet in fifteen lines, just for the sake of being different from others.

Yet George Meredith made use of a sixteen-line form of verse in his *Modern Love,* which is often loosely spoken of as a sonnet sequence—and he was justified in doing so because he knew exactly why he did it. The poem is not merely a series of separate and complete thoughts, connected by a single thread, like pearls strung on the same string, after the fashion of Shakespeare's sonnets, or the *Sonnets from the Portuguese.* They form a continuous piece of narrative, and for that reason the extra two lines help the forward movement, where the formal sestet of the sonnet would have continually broken in with a misplaced sense of finality. Many a rule of rhetoric and prosody and technique may be broken—provided always that you have a reason that justifies you. The early stories of Kipling fairly bristled with strange phrases, words forced into new partnerships, and what Mr. Gosse has called "the noisy, newspaper bustle of his little peremptory sentences." And yet, more often than not, he justified himself, because he knew so well what he was about—and knew also that he was succeeding in expressing his thoughts a little better than they could have been expressed in any other and more conventional way. So remember, in writing, to be independent; on occasion be even boldly innovative, so long as you can be so intelligently.

Chapter 3

# The Author's Purpose

At the moment of beginning this chapter, which is to concern itself with The Author's Purpose, a memory comes back, very clear and distinct, of a certain Sunday many years ago, and of a rather prim old lady who had been to hear an eccentric and sensational preacher, and who came away shaking her head and murmuring in scandalised wonderment: "Why, he didn't even give out a text!" Now, whether the preacher really had dispensed with a text or whether the bewildered old lady had simply lost sight of it is immaterial; what does matter is that in the sermon we have at least one type of composition in which there is a clearly understood convention that the writer's purpose shall be defined beyond all question, and at the very start. In other literary forms, unfortunately, the need of having a purpose is more easily overlooked, because that purpose is more or less disguised, instead of being embodied in a specified chapter and verse. Yet, the mere circumstance that the poet and the novelist, for instance, differ from the preacher in not having to announce in advance the theme of their discourse does not alter the fact that "Beauty is truth, truth beauty" is the text of the *Ode on a Grecian Urn,* and that Owen Wister's *The Virginian* is an eloquent attempt to reconcile the New England conscience to the rude ethics of Western justice.

Now, the average person who might be very quick to note the omission of a Sunday morning text will quite complacently read a novel or a short story that does not possess even a rudimentary central idea without being aware that there is anything wrong with it. But wait until someone happens to ask such a reader what the book he chances to be reading is about. If the answer is crisp and concise you may know without reading it yourself that the book has something in it that is worth while; if, on the contrary, the answer comes uncertainly and long-drawn out, something to the effect that "It is about a man and a girl and they are talking together and a lot of things have happened," and so on indefinitely, you may be pretty sure that the book has no central idea at all.

Now the one way of bringing home to a young writer the necessity of having a definite purpose is to make him form the habit of literary criticism which was urged in the preceding chapter. After we have once learned to ask ourselves regarding each new poem or essay or novel that comes our way: Did the author know what he was trying to do and has he succeeded in doing it?—then we are in a position to know that the most exasperating of all books is that which apparently has no central idea, no definite purpose—the amorphous, jelly-fish type of book that can no more be measured by a definite standard than we can measure a puff of cigarette smoke. And almost equally hopeless is the book in which the author has confused his purposes, leaving us vaguely guessing between several solutions; or, again, the book in which the author's purpose and form are hopelessly out of proportion—either a little tupenny purpose, like a seed pearl buried in a gypsy setting; or else a great big ethical principle squandered on a triolet, like a Koh-i-noor set for a little finger-ring. When we learn to recognise what bad workmanship these fundamental faults produce in others, then we are prepared to lay down the following rules for our own work: that we will always begin with a clearly defined purpose, single, not complex; that this purpose shall receive consistent development from the first line of our work to the last; and that we shall strive for a nicely balanced relationship between our central purpose and the setting we have chosen for it.

It is well, however, to understand at the outset just what we mean by this term, The Author's Purpose. It is used in this chapter in a very broad and elastic sense. It is something far broader than a deliberate intention to teach a lesson or to preach a creed—although these of course are among the subdivisions of the author's purpose. Perhaps the most general, all-embracing definition that may be given is to call it simply the thing which the author has set his heart upon saying, the one main idea that he must get across to his audience, whether he succeeds in saying anything else or not. It comes very near to being synonymous with the germ idea, the nucleus or starting point of the whole work—but for the fact that an author's starting-point, the initial incident, the intuitive flash or whatever it may be that sets him moving along a particular path, may in some special cases be altogether lost to sight by the time he is ready to write his opening sentence.

Now it makes no difference when or where or how a writer stumbles upon the idea which is to serve as his central purpose. It may spring from his head at a moment's notice like Athena, full armoured—as was the case with the late Frank Norris, who, as has often been told, came one morning to his publisher's office, pale and trembling all over with excitement, and gasping out, almost inarticulately, "I've got a big idea A great big idea The biggest idea ever" It was the outlined scheme for his trilogy of the Epic of the Wheat—the trilogy which began with *The Octopus* and *The Pit,* and which poor Norris did not live to round out with *The Wolf.*[1] Or, again, the controlling purpose of a work may not be born until the structure has risen some distance toward completion and the author suddenly discovers that he is building better than he knew. But when this happens he must look carefully to his foundations to see if they be stout enough to bear the weight of the heavier structure. Otherwise it would be better to tear it down, stone from stone, and begin all over again. No thumb rule can be given for the discovery or manufacture of the Author's Purpose. If you find yourself compelled to ask, like the little prince in *Les Rois En Exile, "Donnez moi des idées sur les choses,"* then you had better lay aside your ambition to write.[2] But

---

1. Compare the account given by de Louvenjoul of Balzac's first conception of the idea of bringing together under one title, *La Comedie Humaine,* all the novels he had already published. He hurried to the house of his sister, Mme. Surville, to announce the great event. His sister beheld him enter the parlor with his hat slightly tilted over one ear, his chest thrust out, his walking stick held aloft, like the staff of a drum-major, while from between his lips came a martial "Boom, boom-de-de boom!" and he strode forward in cadenced solemnity, as if he were actually at the head of a regiment. Reaching the sofa where his sister sat, he suddenly came to a halt: then in a tone that was at once grave and comical, he said: "Madam, salute a Genius!"

2. Interesting in this connection is Daudet's own statement of the origin of *Kings in*

perhaps the advice given by Thoreau is as good as any that can be devised for stimulating a sluggish imagination:

> It would be a true discipline for the writer to take the least film of thought that floats in the twilight sky of his mind for his theme, about which he has scarcely one idea (that would be teaching his ideas how to shoot), make a lecture of this, by assiduity and attention get perchance two views of the same, increase a little the stock of knowledge, clear a new field instead of manuring the old.

The great trouble is that ideas, real ideas such as are likely to be of any importance or interest to a considerable number of people, are not so plentiful as to be easily found. They frequently represent well-nigh half the battle in a literary achievement of any importance. It is always so much easier to echo than to originate. One thing is certain: the central idea will not come at command; it must be patiently hoped for, watched for, struggled for; it usually represents a good deal of hard work and a good deal of discouragement. Gibbon, as the whole world knows, received his inspiration for his monumental history one evening in Rome, as he sat musing among the ruins of the Capitol, while the barefooted friars were singing vespers in the Temple of Jupiter. Yet he records, regarding the subsequent writing of his history:

> At the outset, all was dark and doubtful; even the title of the work, the true era of the Decline and Fall of the Empire, the limits of the introduction, the division of the chapters, and the order of the narrative; and I was often tempted to cast away the labour of seven years.

---

*Exile:* "Of all my books this (*Kings in Exile*) is unquestionably the one which I found most difficulty in standing on its feet, the one which I carried longest in my head in the stage of title and vague outline, as it appeared to me one October evening on Place du Carrousal, in the tragic rent in the Parisian sky caused by the fall of the Tuileries.

"Dethroned princes exiling themselves in Paris after their downfall, taking up their quarters on Rue de Rivoli, and when they woke in the morning and raised the shades at their windows, discovering those ruins—such was the first vision of *Kings in Exile*."

The uncertainty, the false start, the work which must be begun anew and on a different plan, have all been rather eloquently generalised by Mr. Henry James in his preface to *The Awkward Age:*

> When I think of my many false measurements that have resulted, after much anguish, in decent symmetries, I find the whole case a theme for the philosopher. The little ideas one wouldn't have treated save for the design of keeping them small, the developed situation that one would never with malice prepense have undertaken, the long stories that had thoroughly meant to be short, the short subjects that had underhandedly plotted to be long, the hypocrisy of modest beginnings, the audacity of misplaced middles, the triumph of intentions never entertained—with these patches, as I look about, I see my experience paved: an experience to which nothing is wanting save some grasp of its final lesson.

Occasionally it may happen that the central idea comes in a sort of miraculous flash, an inspiration, a dream, such as was the case with Stevenson's *Dr. Jekyll and Mr. Hyde:* "In the small hours of one morning," says Mrs. Stevenson," I was awakened by cries of horror from Louis. Thinking he had a nightmare, I awakened him. He said angrily, 'Why did you wake me? I was dreaming a fine bogey tale.' I had awakened him at the first transformation scene." So clearly did Stevenson have his germ idea in mind that the tale was written off in all the white heat of inspiration; yet it is recorded that that first draft had to be destroyed and the work begun anew, because the original plan lacked what we now think of as the underlying idea of the whole story, namely, the dual nature of the hero. In Stevenson's first conception Dr. Jekyll was equally bad at heart in both his natural and his acquired form.

Now it is quite true that the author's purpose, as a question of craftsmanship, concerns no one but himself; but there is one important reservation. The author's purpose must be suited to the literary form in which he chooses to work. He must decide in advance whether he means to be a preacher or an artist; for he cannot successfully be both. If he is a born fighter and his chosen weapons are words, it makes no difference which side of a controversy he espouses; he may fight for Whigs or Tories, slavery or emancipation, Christian Science or the Church of Rome—but to succeed he must put the whole vigour of his personality into it. Polemics can never be successfully made a matter of art for art's sake. On the other hand, in pure literature, whatever private feelings an author may have, whatever bias he may let us guess at, he has no business to intrude it deliberately into his written text. Mr. Frederic Harrison in his *Memories and Thoughts* has expressed this same important truth in a way that makes for remembrance:

> Mark Pattison, of Oxford, used to say to a pupil who happens now to be both a brilliant writer and a leading statesman: "My good friend, you are not the stuff of which men of letters are made. You want to make people do something or you want to teach something. That is fatal to pure literature."
>
> Once or twice in my life I have taken up the pen in a vein of literary exercise, as a man turns to a game of billiards or to gardening after his day's work. But the demon soon arises and I find myself in earnest, trying to bring men over to one side. It is hopeless to make a man of letters out of a temper like that. Literature is art, and the artist should never preach.[1]

And similarly Marion Crawford in his little monograph on *The Novel: What It Is,* writes as follows:

> In art of all kinds the moral lesson is a mistake. It is one thing to exhibit an ideal worthy to be imitated, though inimitable in all its perfection, but so clearly noble as to appeal directly to the sympathetic string that hangs untuned in the dullest heart;

---

1. And Lord Macaulay, writing of poetry in his *Essay on Milton,* comes curiously near saying the same thing in slightly different words: "Analysis is not the business of the poet. His office is to portray, not to dissect. His creed . . . will no more influence his poetry, properly so called, than the notions which a painter may have conceived respecting the lachrymal glands or the circulation of the blood will affect the tears of his Niobe or the blushes of his Aurora. If Shakespeare had written a book on the motives of human actions, it is by no means certain that it would have been a good one."

to make man brave without arrogance, woman pure without prudishness, love enduring yet earthly, not angelic, friendship sincere but not ridiculous. It is quite another matter to write a "guide to morality," or a "handbook for practical sinners" and call either one a novel, no matter how much fiction it may contain. Wordsworth tried the moral lesson and spoiled some of his best work with botany and the Bible.

It is the disregard of this important axiom of literature that has produced that hybrid monstrosity, the so-called Novel-with-a-Purpose. Of all the purposes which by any chance may actuate a writer the most mistaken purpose and the one most destructive to good art is that of forcibly bringing people over to think as he does by a deliberate and conscienceless distortion of life as we see it around us. There was not merely a degree of grotesqueness in the old-fashioned Sunday-school story of the good little boy who had plum pudding and the bad little boy who went fishing and was drowned. There was an immorality about it as well, the immorality that always attaches to a deliberate perversion of our experiences of life. And the same immorality attaches to any novelist who takes upon himself the privilege of the Deity and says "Vengeance is mine," forgetful of the fact that in this world at least rewards and punishments of human acts are meted out quite inexorably in accordance with the laws of nature.

Having digressed to this extent upon the special subject of the purpose novel, we must in. fairness go a little further in order to make clear a distinction about which a good deal of confusion exists in the minds of many readers and writers. It may be defined as the distinction between the Novel-with-a-Purpose, on the one hand, and the Author-with-a-Purpose, on the other. There is no logical reason why an author should not have the strongest sort of prejudices, convictions, enthusiasms; only, he must not be trying to force them down the reader's throat. He may believe, like Harriet Beecher Stowe, that slavery is a crime; he may agree with Zola that race suicide is a national menace. A sincere belief of that sort is the surest guarantee of powerful workmanship, so long as the author records only what he sees, so long as he remembers that life itself is the most potent teacher of its own lessons. But so soon as he becomes mistrustful or impatient of life and tries dishonestly to magnify the facts and distort statistics, then his book becomes a Novel-with-a-Purpose, more potent to antagonise than to convince. A good object lesson on the distinction between the Novel-with-a-Purpose and the Author-with-a-Purpose is afforded by the Russians. Owing to Russian censorship writers with strong doctrines to preach found themselves driven to the form of fiction as the only vehicle in which the lessons they wished to teach could reach the public. But they were wise enough to recognise that the existing conditions around them, the conditions they were most eager to correct, would speak for themselves without any perversion or interference in their part. As Mr. Howells in *My Literary Passions* forcefully puts it:

> When I remembered the deliberate and impatient moralising of Thackeray, the clumsy exegesis of George Eliot, the knowing nods and winks of Charles Reade, the stage-carpeting and limelighting of Dickens, and even the fine and impotent analysis of Hawthorne, it was with a joyful enthusiasm that I realised the great art of Tourguenief . . . here was a master who was apparently not trying to work out a plot, who was not even trying to work out a character, but was standing aside from the whole affair and letting the characters work the plot out.

But whatever a writer's purpose may be, and whatever type of literature he has chosen in which to express it, he has got to do something more than idly say to himself one fine day, "I think I will write (let us say) a sonnet about a pearl, or a novel about the beef trust"—and then on another fine day formulates his first line or his opening sentence without the slightest idea what is coming next or where he eventually proposes to arrive. He must take the time and trouble to sit down and work out in detail just precisely what he is trying to do and what is the best way of doing it. It is not only in the department of the drama that a scenario is indispensable. Every piece of writing that aspires to be anything more than ephemeral is as much in need of a detailed ground plan as a Gothic cathedral or a modern office building. All beginners who cherish the dangerous fallacy that a masterpiece of prose or verse can be flung off in a white heat of inspiration would do well to commit to memory a large part of Poe's essay on *The Philosophy of Composition,* of which the following are perhaps the most weighty and apposite paragraphs:

> Most writers—poets in especial—prefer to have it understood that they compose by a species of fine frenzy—an ecstatic intuition; and would positively shudder at letting the public take a peep behind the scenes at the elaborate and vacillating conditions of thought, at the true purposes seized only at the last moment, at the innumerable glimpses of ideas that arrived not at the maturity of full view, at the fully matured fancies discarded in despair as unmanageable, at the cautious selection and rejection, at the painful erasures and interpolations—in a word, at the wheels and pinions, the tackle of scene-shifting, the step-ladders and demon-traps, the cock's feathers, the red paint and the black patches, which in ninety-nine cases out of the hundred constitute the properties of the literary *histrio.*

> For my own part, I have neither sympathy with the repugnance alluded to, nor at any time the least difficulty in recalling to mind the progressive steps of any of my compositions; and since the interest of an analysis or reconstruction, such as I have considered a *desideratum,* is quite independent of any real or fancied interest in the things analysed, it will not be regarded as a breach of decorum on my part to show the *modus operandi* by which some one of my own works was put together. I select *The Raven* as most generally known. It is my design to render it manifest that no one point in its *composition* is referable either to accident or intuition; that the work proceeded step by step to its completion with the precision and rigid consequence of a mathematical problem.

Poe, of course, is an extreme case. A poem or a story that develops with the rigid consequence of a mathematical problem is necessarily too artificial to pass as a transcript from life. But a study of Poe's analysis of *The Raven*—quite aside from the question whether he actually wrote the poem, as he says he did, or merely succeeded in making himself think he did so[1]—compels us to face, for ourselves, in all our own work, the artistic demand for unity of effect, simplicity of means, singleness of purpose. Learn to do as much as possible of the sheer drudgery of composition at the start; every hour spent in careful drafting should save two in the actual writing. An extreme case which none the less is a case in point, is contained in the following anecdote given by Mr. A. E. Davidson in his *Life of Alexandre Dumas:*

> Dumas often declared that, when once he had mapped out in his mind the scheme of a novel or a play, the work was practically accomplished, since the mere writing of it presented no difficulty, and could be performed as fast as the pen could travel. Someone begged leave to dispute this assertion, and the result was a wager. Dumas had at that time in his head the plan of the *Chevalier de Maison Rouge,* of which he had not yet written a word, and he now made a bet of one hundred louis with his sceptical friend that he would write the first volume of the novel in seventy-two hours (including the time for meals and sleep). The volume was to be formed by seventy-five large foolscap pages, each page containing forty-five lines and each line fifty letters. In sixty-six hours Dumas had done the work—3375 lines—in his fair, flowing hand, disfigured by no erasures—and the bet was won with six hours to spare.

Dumas, however, was a striking exception in being able to dispense with revision. Alternate elimination and expansion is the method by which great works of literature have usually reached their final form—and it is far easier to expand and cut, expand and cut again, in the mere rough outline than in the fully developed book. Don't shirk your plot construction—and here I am using the phrase in an all-embracing sense—an essay or a sermon deserves careful plotting as much as a novel—plot construction is a wholesome discipline; and while there is not one chance in a hundred that you will overdo it,

---

1. Poe wrote the *Raven,* later the genesis of this *Raven.* This—the afterstroke—American pleasantry, no doubt, but admired and emulated by our young school. The devil of the thing is to find the raven, the dry sob, the foreboding nevermore.—DAUDET, *Notes from Life.*

there is every chance that you will all the time be teaching yourself some new and useful trick, some clever short-cut, some way of knitting your whole structure more firmly together. It would be well if every young writer were to reduce to a ten-word limit his central idea before even starting to plot his story; keep those ten words inscribed upon a cardboard, hanging above his desk, and ask himself, with each incident, each character, each shift of scene, "To what degree does this help on my central idea? Is it essential, or only a digression? If not actually related, has it a symbolic significance that justifies it structurally? In any case, is it the best, the very last and best thing I can do?" If not, then cut it out ruthlessly and try again, and yet again, until you are sure that the best of which you are capable is found.

Of course, it is quite easy for someone to object that many of the greatest masters of the past have not composed in this manner; that Fielding and Smollett, Dickens and Thackeray were notoriously loose in plot construction, and that Trollope him-. self acknowledges, "I have never troubled myself about the construction of plots and am not now insisting on thoroughness in a branch of work in which I myself have not been very thorough." And the objector might go a step further and ask: Did Shakespeare, when he was writing *Hamlet,* inscribe above his desk, "To be or not to be, that is the question," as a reminder that his theme was the tragedy of a vacillating nature; or similarly, when he wrote *Othello,* "A man not easily jealous but, when roused, perplexed in the extreme"; or again for *Macbeth,* "Vaulting ambition that o'erleaps itself, and falls on the other"? And of course the answer is obvious enough: that the masters of literature are great enough to break the rules; that had Shakespeare constructed as Ibsen did, English literature would have been robbed of some of its noblest lines; and that when we speak of the craftsmanship of writing we are speaking of rules that must be mastered before one has earned the right to break them.

Remember, also, in choosing the authors who are to be your models, to exercise discrimination regarding the particular qualities that you will copy from each of them. Go to Dickens and Thackeray for character drawing, if you choose, but not for plot. And similarly, remember that Trollope was able to say of his characters:

There is a gallery of them, and of all that gallery I may say that I know the tone of the voice, and the colour of the hair, every flame of the eye, and the very clothes they wear. Of each man I could assert whether he would have said these words or the other words; of every woman, whether she would then have smiled or so have frowned. When I shall feel that this intimacy ceases, then I shall know that the old horse should be turned out to grass.

But if you want a model of careful construction from among the early novelists, you can do no better than turn to Hawthorne. "Hawthorne's method," says Andrew Lang, "is revealed in his published note-books. In them he jotted the germ of an idea, the first notion of a singular, perhaps supernatural situation. Many of these he never used at all; on others he would dream and dream till the persons in the situations became characters and the thing was evolved into a story. Thus he may have invented such a problem as this: 'The effect of a great, sudden sin on a simple and joyous nature,' and thence came all the substance of *The Marble Faun.*" As a matter of fact, *The Marble Faun* is a very wonderful example of close construction admirably disguised. It has all the effect of a vast canvas, a prodigality of material in character, and incident, and panoramic scene; but under examination, it reveals little by little the nice balance of all its parts, the rigid economy of its means, the fine art that has subordinated every part to a consistent development of the central idea, a conservation of the unity of purpose.

Second only in importance to having a purpose is the necessity of clothing that purpose in a suitable form. Some themes lend themselves to a variety of different treatments. A great war may give us both an epic and an *opera-bouffe,* an *Iliad* and *La Belle Helene.* The sin of intemperance finds expression at one time in a *L'Assommoir* and at another in a *Tam O'Shanter.* And in general the rule may be laid down, that the form in which any central idea is to be clothed depends less upon the idea than upon the individual ability of the author. But the practical distinction of this is really not great. You may have conceived some light, frothy little idea, such as would make a graceful triolet; it makes no difference whether a triolet is the biggest thing lurking in that idea, or whether someone else might take it and develop it into something of much greater dignity—in either case it is an error of judgment on your part to give that little idea the misplaced dignity of an elegy or a sonnet. Or perhaps you have hit upon a really big situation deserving of the broad treatment of a Hardy or a Meredith; if you are able to see it in that broad, big way be careful not to squander it on a short story or hammock novel, no matter how many other writers might, with more limited vision, have chosen to do the smaller thing.

Just precisely what literary form is the best possible form in which to clothe a central idea is another of those many things that cannot be taught, because it is so peculiarly personal to each writer. My own conviction is that it is something largely instinctive; that a short-story theme usually presents itself to the mind in the first instance as a short story, a dramatic theme as a drama, and the material for a long novel as a long novel and nothing else. The Anglo-Saxon writer, however, both in England and America, is very largely a writer of one or at most two literary forms. This is in marked contrast to the Continental habit. In France and Italy it is quite in the ordinary course of things for a young writer to begin with a volume of verse,[1] follow it up with collected essays, usually of literary criticism, then a novel or two, a four-act play—and at that time he has reached a point where he feels at liberty to confine himself to whichever form he finds most congenial. A man with this sort of training may, of course, have wasted himself to some extent in misplaced efforts, in attempting certain things for which he was not temperamentally fitted; but he seldom makes the mistake of trying to fit an idea into the wrong literary framework. It is the other type of craftsman, so common in this country: the man who starts with a fixed idea that he is to be a dramatist and nothing else, or a lyric poet and nothing else, or an essay writer and nothing else—who is all the time trying to force his ideas into a shape for which they were not meant. If, for

---

1. "Maupassant began by writing verses; that seems to be the rule, the versified form being the inevitable one for the dawn of literature and for the budding writer as well. Nearly all the masters of contemporary prose have begun by writing verse, even M. Alexandre Dumas himself. Later they have proved their critical taste by not repeating the experiment"—Rene Doumic, Essay on Maupassant.

instance, a man cannot and will not write anything but a sonnet; if he is unable to think in any other terms than those of a sonnet, then whenever an idea comes to him that is not a sonnet idea, he must either reject it altogether or else produce a sonnet that had better not have been written. For these reasons it cannot be too forcibly urged upon young writers to keep their minds open by the practice of several different forms at once. You are sure to be eventually a better dramatist for having had some practice in narrative fiction; and you will probably write a better short story if you have occasionally done a little literary criticism. There is more common sense than appears on the surface in the casual confession by Mr. A. C. Benson in his lightful volume *From a College Window:*

> The two things I have found to be of infinite service to myself in learning to write prose have been keeping a full diary and writing poetry.

It is interesting to remember in this connection that George Meredith once wrote:

> Writing for the stage would be a corrective of a too incrusted scholarly style, into which some great ones fall at times. It keeps minor writers to a definite plan and English.

In other words, in literature as well as in life there are some occasions when the longest way round is the shortest way home, and one of them is the art of acquiring a particular branch of literary form by the practice of forms that are radically different.

Chapter 4

# The Technique of Form

There are few of us who have not, at one time or another, been
drawn into the childish pastime of attempting to trace a pig with our
eyes blindfolded. We usually began bravely enough by drawing two
fairly symmetrical ears, and if the pencil was not quite as steady as it
might have been, as it proceeded to delineate the snout, the general
effect was rather creditable; at least, the bystanders had not yet
found adequate cause for merriment. But when it came to the legs,
our sense of proportion weakened, wavered, slipped utterly from us;
those four legs straggled across the paper in riotous disorder like the
distortions of a convex mirror, the pencil wobbled more and more
hopelessly and the last mad dash for the finish landed, as likely as
not, in the middle of the fore leg instead of at the starting point, the
tail curled in a fantastic corkscrew from the middle of the back, and
the eye, added as an afterthought, gazed at us in a detached sort of
way some inches from the rest of the drawing. All this may seem
irrelevant to the Craftsmanship of Writing, but unfortunately it is not.
One of the commonest experiences in a critic's ordinary routine is
to come across literary efforts of various form and magnitude which
convey the impression that they too have been constructed with the
eyes blindfolded.[1] The main, difference is that the general effect is
more saddening than ludicrous. And the reason for this, of course, is

---

1. Writers should remember Carlyle's advice: "To the poet, as to every other, we say,
first of all, *See*. If you cannot do that, it is of no use to keep stringing rhymes together,
jingling sensibilities against each other, and name yourself a *poet;* there is no hope for
you."

that there is nothing especially discreditable to the average man or woman to be unable to draw a pig with their eyes blindfolded, while for the literary craftsman to be careless and slovenly in his technique of form is not only discreditable but without excuse.

Now, having introduced this metaphor of the pig, let us go a step further and find out clearly to what extent it applies to the literary craftsman. There is no hard and fast rule regarding form, whether we are speaking of drawing a pig or writing a short story; in either process there is ample latitude for individual expression—there is no such absolute uniformity required as in minting a gold eagle or moulding a Rogers group. Your literary or artistic pig may be fat or lean, contented or disgruntled, small, round and pink, or razor-backed and black and bristling—but you have no right to take liberties with his recognised anatomical structure—draw any kind of a pig you choose, so long as it remains a pig. In other words, you have no right to profess to be working in a certain recognised literary form, and then so distort the leading characteristics of that form that it becomes something entirely different. "The confusion of kinds," says Henry James, "is the inelegance of letters and the stultification of values."

It goes not by any means follow that an author is not free to invent new literary forms or varieties, if he has the inventive power. There is no rule in art forbidding the unusual, the new or even the grotesque. There is no reason why we should not have, from time to time, something undreamed of in the philosophy of literary form, any more than there is a reason why the sculptor should not carve a griffin out of stone, although he never saw a griffin in the flesh. Otherwise we should have been deprived of some of the most interesting experiments in English literature: *Gulliver's Travels,* and *Pilgrim's Progress,* the *De Coverley Papers, Alice's Adventures,* the *Jungle Books,* and *Redcoat Captain*—the list could be prolonged indefinitely. But any writer who wishes to discard the accepted forms and make new forms for himself would do well to remember what Ruskin said regarding the difference between the Lombard griffin and the classical griffin, in his chapter on the Grotesque:

"Well, but," the reader says, "what do you mean by calling

*either* of them true? There never were such beasts in the world as either of these."

No, never; but the difference is, that the Lombard workman did really see a griffin in his imagination, and carved it from the life, meaning to declare to all ages that he had verily seen with his immortal eyes such a griffin as that; but the classical workman never saw a griffin at all, nor anything else; but put the whole thing together by line and rule.

In other words, if a writer is big enough, inspired enough—call it what you will—to see with his immortal eyes some new and better form, then let him use it fearlessly, provided that he is quite sure that it is a new form and not a distorted old one. For it is a much rarer and harder thing to produce a glorified griffin than a misshapen pig.

Yet the necessity of studying the technique of form in all its minutest details is so little understood and so slowly grasped by the average beginner in writing that it is a temptation to insist upon its paramount importance even to the point of tediousness. So many young writers have their answer all pat: What, they ask, is the use of putting so much stress on form? The great writers of the past were notoriously loose and careless in construction; look at the rambling, episodic character of Homer and Cervantes and Rabelais; and were Fielding and Thackeray and Dickens much better in their technique of plot? Of course, all this is perfectly true; and the chief reason why so many young writers—and older ones, too, for that matter—are slow to appreciate the importance of good technique, is the conservative force of tradition—the great masters of the past, who wrote before the more elaborate technique of today had been developed, did thus and so; and if good enough for them, why not, is the argument, good enough for us? No less a person than the Spanish novelist, Senor Valdes, betrays in this regard a curious lack of critical acumen: The Latin races, he grants, are accustomed to give greater attention to unity of structure; the Anglo-Saxons and the Slays, on the contrary, prefer a greater variety of interest, a more prodigal abundance of life:

One of the best contemporary Russian novels, War and Peace, might with very little effort be divided in two, because it contains two perfectly defined actions, which are carried on side by side throughout the whole course of the book: Which of these conceptions of the composition of a novel is the true one? In my opinion, both of them. To decide in favour of one of them would be to assert the inferiority of the novels written according to the other—and that seems to me unjust. Dickens, Thackeray, Gogol, Tolstoy are as excellent novelists as Balzac, George Sand, Flaubert and Manzoni.[1]

The fallacy of Senor Valdes's argument, of course, is his failure to recognise that while the English and Russian novelists whom he names are as great, if not greater, than the French and Italian, their greatness is not due to their looser method of construction, but in spite of it. There is progress in the art of writing, as well as in other arts, and the wise modern writer profits by the improved methods. The tales of Boccaccio are inimitable specimens of their kind; but now that we have the modern conception of what a short story should be, as formulated by Poe and Mau-passant and Kipling, it would seem scarcely worth while for any writer of today deliberately to revert to the cruder form of the early Italian *novella*. Balzac's *Contes Drolatiques* are likely to remain the last attempt of the sort to gain literary recognition. *Don Quixote* is one of the three or four indisputably greatest books in the world—but that is no reason why any twentieth-century tyro in novel writing should take Cervantes for his model and imitate successfully all his faults of construction, while the magic that makes the book unique forever eludes it imitators.

It seems inevitable that in discussing the technique of form the argument should tend constantly to revert to prose rather than poetry, and to the novel in preference to all other prose forms. And it is quite natural that this should be so. The necessity of structure in verse is in a way axiomatic; it enters into the very definition. In short, in all verse, from the greatest to the least, there is something which may not unjustly be called architectural in the way it is built. Indeed, the more formal types, like the rondeau, the ballade, the rondel, the sonnet, offer to the eye, as they lie upon the printed

---

1. From preface to *La Hermana San Sulpicio*.

page, as definite a suggestion of a ground plan as any blue print of the modern draughtsman. The regularity of recurring rhymes, the marshalled lines of numbered syllables and stresses inevitably suggest the methodical courses of brick and masonry, the stately rows of Doric columns or Gothic pinnacles. Every great epic is a temple in words, every nursery rhyme a structure of toy blocks, playthings of uncomprehending merriment. Carlyle was not the first writer to liken the *Divine Comedy* to a cathedral; but no one has ever worded it so well:

> A true inward symmetry, what we call an architectural harmony, reigns in it, proportionates it all; . . . the three kingdoms, Inferno, Purgatorio, Paradiso, look out on one another like compartments of a great edifice; a great, supernatural world-cathedral piled up there, stern, solemn, awful; Dante's World of Souls!

Now in prose, and especially in fiction, which enjoys the advantage of being the most elastic of all literary forms, the architectural element is far less in evidence, because the best technique in fiction demands the most careful framework, most carefully disguised. But, supposing that a young writer says quite frankly, "I recognise the truth of all you say; I believe in the importance of the Technique of Form, and I want to learn and obey the rules of the best construction. If I try to write a novel, I want it to be a novel in the best sense, and not a string of short stories. If I write a short story, I want to feel sure that it is truly a short story in spirit and inherent purpose, as well as in outward form. But how am I to decide what particular artistic form is best adapted to be my medium of expression? What I want to write is (let us say) a novel; but are my ideas big enough? Are they inherently long-story ideas, or are they foredoomed never to be anything more than short stories?" This point was touched upon briefly in the preceding chapter; but it is so extremely important to the individual writer, and a miscomprehension of it has led so many beginners astray, that a certain amount of repetition seems justifiable, especially as it paves the way to another thought of some importance.

The greatest mistake that a young writer can make is that of thinking of ideas as being in any sense a lot of square pegs that must not be placed in round holes, or *vice versa*. An idea is not foreordained to any exclusive appropriation by any one artistic form; it is not inevitably the beginning of a sonnet or of a four-act drama, any more than a ball of yarn is necessarily destined, as it comes from the spinning-wheel, either for an afghan or a pair of stockings. Ideas are the raw material of literature; what they are to be worked into, depends not upon the ideas themselves, but upon the individual author's bent of mind, the way in which his thoughts naturally take shape. We are too apt to think of a thought, a really big and important thought, as we think of a precious stone, something crystallised and unyielding, something which can be cut and polished, to be sure, but only in accordance with its natural angles and lines of cleavage. We would come nearer the truth if we likened ideas to pure gold in the ingot, that may be worked into any shape, applied to any purpose, forming the standard of value in the world of letters, yet capable of being spread out to infinitesimal thinness, in order to give cheapness the glitter of a spurious worth. What is wrought from the ingot depends upon the skill and genius of the goldsmith; it is not the fault of the elemental gold, if, instead of delicate miracles of the jeweller's art, it finds itself debased to an electro bath for Ten-Cent Store cuff-buttons!

It follows that we can do no poorer service to a young writer than to persuade him that an idea which he has already seen clearly in one form, must not be used in that form, but for something quite different. We sometimes hear a young poet receive advice, somewhat after this fashion: "Yes, the idea that you have in mind for a sonnet is a good idea in itself, but the trouble with it is that it is not a sonnet idea; it never could make a good sonnet; give it up!" It always seemed to me that it must take an uncommon amount of boldness to assume such a responsibility as that! The utmost that anyone has a right to say is, "That is an idea from which I, myself, could not make a good sonnet; I, individually, cannot see it in the sonnet form," or, perhaps, if the intimacy between the adviser and would-be poet justifies this attitude: "From what I know of your previous work, I cannot believe that you could give this particular idea the adequate treatment and development for a sonnet; give it up, not on account of the idea's limitations, but because of your own." But the usual and safe rule is that every writer must find out for himself what shape he may best give his ideas—and that is why it is generally wiser, if a writer has critical friends whose advice he values, to get his start by himself, have his first draught finished, or at least well advanced, before asking for a critical opinion. It often happens that an idea which, when presented in the rough, seems to the critic quite hopeless, becomes with even a slight degree of working-up, not only promising, but triumphantly vindicated. Think how absurd it would sound to say to a goldsmith: "Don't try to make a ring out of that piece of gold wire; there isn't a ring in that wire, there is nothing but a scarf-pin!" Yet that is precisely the sort of misleading advice that is not infrequently given to story writers. Many an author has wasted months on a bad novel, when he could have used the same idea in a good short story; many a short story has spoiled an idea that might have served for a ballad or an elegy, or a musical comedy—not because there was any incongruity in the ideas themselves, but because the author failed to follow his natural bent.

But, whatever form a young writer uses, it is his first duty to master the technique of that form, to familiarise himself with its entire history, to learn not only how the best authors have used that form in the past, but also how the modern generation is modifying it today. I am continually amazed at being asked by beginners, "Isn't it better for me to read as little as possible of contemporary books? Am I not in danger of losing my originality if I fill my mind with the ideas of others? Is it not bad for my style to read any books except the recognised classics? "Personally, I have little patience with such an attitude of mind. The man or woman who has so little originality or inventive power as to be bewildered, stunted, overwhelmed by contact with the thoughts of others, offers a rather hopeless case anyhow; the great majority of normal human beings find something stimulating rather than deadening in wide reading; and to the craftsman who is really interested in his art it must be a very hopeless book indeed that does not give him something upon which to whet his inventive faculty. The very imperfections of a plot in any current penny-dreadful may suggest, by the glaring way in which an opportunity is missed, a new twist that might be given—and so you have the starting point of a new and perhaps a big story. And in any case a writer cannot afford to be ignorant of what is being done today in his own field. Such neglect is only a few degrees worse than for a lawyer to refuse to recognise the authority of a case decided later than 1850, or for a physician to ignore modern methods of treating disease, lest he should lose the originality of his own methods. The comparison is not quite so far-fetched as perhaps at first sight it may seem. The fact that there were some brilliant surgeons half a century ago in no way minimises the importance of the antiseptic methods of today; and the inclusion of *Tom Jones* and *Roderick Random* and *Tristram Shandy* among the English classics does not alter the fact that there exists today a technique of fiction such as was not remotely dreamed of by Sterne or Smollett or Fielding. One of the first things for a beginner to learn, if he would master the technique of form, is to distinguish between the writers who have already mastered it and those who have become great in spite of poor technique. It is the difference between a rough diamond and a polished rhinestone—the value may lie wholly in the stone or wholly in the cutting. But best of all is the author who combines a flawless technique with the greatness of genius—a perfect cutting and a perfect stone.

For the sake of being specific, let us take one or two examples: for instance, the case of a young writer who wishes to learn the best way in which to write sonnets. Here, as everywhere else, there is a certain measure of the art which cannot be taught. If he has not the inborn instinct that will tell him what thoughts are beautiful and what are not; if he has not a natural sense of harmony that will distinguish between a pleasing sequence of sounds and a discord, it is rather futile to try to help him. But, granted that he possesses these elemental and indispensable qualities, the first thing to do, of course, is to put him in the way of knowing what a sonnet is. Now, the shortest and simplest—I was on the point of saying, the laziest—way to do this would be to pick out some one or two of the great English sonnets, Milton's sonnet on his blindness, or Wordsworth's sonnet to Milton, and say to him: "Here is your model; study the verse scheme and try to do something like it." And of course the student in question would be no more fitted for writing a sonnet than a child is prepared to read when it has mastered only the letter *a*. What he ought to do is to learn the history of the sonnet, to study the development of its form with all permissible variations of rhyme, in Italian as well as in English; to know in what respect the Shakespearean sonnets differ from those of Milton, and his again from Keats or Rossetti. He should know what constitutes a perfectly regular sonnet and what are its pardonable irregularities. Then, and not till then, he is qualified to pass judgment upon a sonnet, either his own or those of others—and, it may be, is capable of producing a sonnet good enough to be given to the world at large.

Or let us take another and far commoner case, that of the would-be writer whose interest lies mainly in fiction. It does not matter whether he prefers the short-story form or that of the novel; his training in either case will be practically the same. What he needs most is a patient study of the authors who have paid strict attention to the technique of form: in English, Henry James and Mr. Howells, Kipling and Hewlett, Gissing and George Moore are only a few whose methods when properly understood are full of illuminating suggestion. And the French are in this respect especially helpful, far more so than the Russians: Turgeneff himself is reported by Henry James to have confessed frankly in conversation that one fault of his own work was "*que cela manque d'architecture.* But," he added, "I would rather, I think, have too little architecture than too much—when there is danger of its interfering with my measure of the truth. The French of course like more of it than I give—having by their own genius such a hand for it; and indeed one must give all one can." There are probably no two novelists to whom the architecture, the underlying and hidden framework of the plot, means precisely the same thing, or who have anything like the same method of developing it. Each writer must learn by experience what method brings him individually the best results. One man may prefer to carry the rough outline of the plot in his head; another can do nothing without an elaborate scenario; a third prefers a diagram, with lines crossing and intercrossing, to show the points at which the lives of the different characters intersect. Nothing would be more helpful than a collection of confessions from our leading novelists as to just how their plots were built up, step by step. Here, for instance, is a curious sidelight from Henry James's preface to *The Awkward Age,* that has already given several suggestive illustrations to these articles:

I remember that in sketching my project (*The Awkward Age*) I drew on a sheet of paper . . . the neat figure of a circle consisting of a number of small rounds disposed at equal distances about a central object. The central object was my situation, to which the thing would owe its title, and the small rounds represented so many distinct lamps, as I liked to call them, the function of each of which would be to light with all due intensity one of its aspects. . . . Each of my "lamps" would be the light of a "single social occasion" in the history and intercourse of the characters concerned, and would bring out to the full the latent colour of the scene in question, and cause it to illustrate, to the last drop, its bearing on my theme.

The whole world knows Emile Zola's elaborate system of "documentation," the long and toilsome preparation that he went through before writing even the first paragraph of his opening chapter. If, for instance, he was going to write a novel on the life of the theatre, so he once told that indefatigable Italian traveller and story teller, Edmondo de Amicis, he would begin by jotting down all that he could remember of his own personal experience in regard to plays and playwrights, theatrical managers and actors; he would then secure all the books he could find that bore upon the subject, would consult friends regarding their experiences, carefully noting down all the details and anecdotes they could give him. Then he would secure letters of introduction to leading members of the theatrical world, spending long hours in the Green Room and at rehearsals, saturating himself with the spirit and the atmosphere of the stage. And out of all this, the plot would little by little take form, almost unconsciously.

According to Zola, this method was by no means peculiar to himself, but was very much the method of Alphonse Daudet as well; and Daudet himself has told frankly of a certain little green notebook from whose pages came *Numa Roumestan* and certain other stories besides. But unlike Zola, Daudet admitted that he could not always control the details of his plots and that there were times when the story took the matter into its own hands, in spite of him. Speaking, for instance, of the criticism against the commonplace death from consumption of one of the characters in *Numa Roumestan,* he gives the following explanation:

But why consumptive? Why that sentimental and romantic death, that commonplace contrivance to arouse the reader's emotion? Why, because one has no control over his work; because, during its gestation, when the idea is tempting us and haunting us, a thousand things become involved in it, dragged to the surface and gathered en route, at the pleasure of the hazards of life, as sea-weed becomes entangled in the meshes of a net. When I was carrying Numa in my brain I was sent to take the waters at Allevard; and there, in the public rooms, I saw youthful faces, drawn, wrinkled, as if carved with a knife; I heard poor, expressionless, husky voices, hoarse coughs, followed by the same furtive movement with the handkerchief or the glove, looking for the red spot at the corner of the lips. Of those pallid, impersonal ghosts, one took shape in my book, as if in spite of me, with the melancholy curriculum of the watering place and its lovely pastoral surroundings, and it has all remained there.

It is somewhat difficult to give general advice regarding the best way to study the technique of form in fiction. The method of diagramming is certainly full of suggestive surprises. I have myself gained some rather happy results in the way of discovering, where one of my lines trailed off into space like a lost comet, that the particular character which that line represented had little or no structural importance in the story. But to a good many writers the diagram method would be of infinitely more trouble than help. To them I would give the more general advice, to try and think of their art in terms of painting; to think of the story they have to tell as being a picture that they are to put upon canvas; and that, like any other picture, it must be subject to the ordinary laws of perspective—all of which has been quite admirably expressed in the following paragraph by Trollope:

"But," the young novelist will say, "with so many pages to be filled, how shall I succeed if I thus confine myself? How am I to know beforehand what space this story of mine will require?. . . If I may not be discursive should the occasion require, how shall I complete my task? The painter suits the size of his canvas to his subject, and must I in my art stretch my subject to my canvas? "This must undoubtedly be done by the novelist; and if he will learn his business, may be done without injury to his effect. He may not paint different pictures on the same canvas, which he will do if he allows himself to wander away to matters outside his own story; but by studying proportion in his work, he may teach himself so to tell his story that it shall naturally fall into the required length. Though his story should be all one, yet it may have many parts. Though the plot itself may require but few characters, it may be so enlarged as to find its full development in many. There may be subsidiary plots, which shall all tend to the elucidation of the main story, and which will take their places as part of one and the same work—as there may be many figures on a canvas which shall not to the spectator seem to form themselves into separate pictures.

Now, if you cultivate the habit of thinking of fiction in the terms of painting, the first question that you are likely to ask of each book that you read is: At what point did the artist set up his easel; from what angle did he see his story? Did he look down upon his little world from some high eminence with the all-seeing eye of Omniscience; or did he deliberately limit the range of vision to a definite angle, a single street or room, or only so much of life as falls beneath the eyes of one of his own / characters? When the technique of fiction was in its infancy, these various methods were indiscriminately used; but now we demand of an author first of all that he shall be consistent. If he professes to tell us, as Mr. James did, What Maisie Knew, we would have a perfect right to resent being told anything that Maisie did not know; if we are to see a story solely from the outside point of view—and Verga's *Cavalleria Rusticana* is probably as perfectly consistent a piece of work of that sort as was ever produced, being so wholly objective that it has the effect of a moving-picture, then we might resent with equal right any attempt to get inside of a character's brain and to tell us what he is thinking of. Secondly, having found out the author's point of view, we want to ask ourselves what the size of his canvas is: how big a story he has to tell and what are his dimensions in point of time as well as space. There are a hundred ways of telling any story. Don't make the mistake of assuming that the author has necessarily chosen the best way. You are entitled to your own opinion; try to find out for yourself just why he began his story where he did, why he spread it over a certain range of days and of miles, why he had nine characters instead of eleven, or fifty-seven instead of forty-three—in other words, when dealing with a modern novel by an author whose technique is supposedly good, cultivate the habit of assuming that the novel contains nothing, not even of the most trivial character, that was not the result of some deliberate purpose, carefully calculated to play its part in the design of the book as a whole. Unfortunately, you will run across many things in the novels of even the best craftsmen that are not the result of any such careful planning; and you will even more frequently find carefully planned effects which have failed of their purpose. And whenever you do run across a clear case of miscalculation, congratulate yourself upon your discovery; for you can generally learn a more valuable and lasting lesson from the blunder of a better craftsman than yourself than you can from a dozen of the same writer's successes.

Yet all this advice is quite futile if the student of craftsmanship cannot bring to his task a certain degree of intelligence and plodding patience. A sort of half understanding of the authors you study becomes that dangerous thing which we are told is the penalty attached at all times to a little knowledge. Unintelligent imitation will often render grotesque what would otherwise have been a really good piece of work. A short time ago a manuscript came into my hands of a story carefully, written, full of a glow of verbal colour and up to a certain point not without interest. It was plain that the writer had saturated himself with the imaginative stores of the French school, such as Prosper Merimee's *Venus D'Ille* and Gautier's *Pied de Momie*. He had caught the trick of telling a story which apparently was due to supernatural causes, yet could, if the reader preferred, be explained on simple and rational grounds. The story was somewhat after this sort: there was a fantastic piece of jewelry from which a single gem was missing; the jewelry was undoubtedly of great antiquity and it possessed mysterious properties calculated to inspire both curiosity and awe. The missing gem is recovered under curious circumstances, and no sooner is it replaced than the possessor forthwith goes into a trance and witnesses very vividly a painful tragedy re-enacted from the vanished centuries.

All this would have been very well indeed but for one trifling mistake; the historical scene that is re-enacted in the vision was (let us say) the death of Julius Caesar, following without variation the traditional account. Of course, as a mystery story, the purpose was defeated. The moment the name Caesar was mentioned the reader knew what to expect and there was no surprise held in reserve. By way of contrast and to show how a story based upon a perfectly familiar historical incident may be handled in order not only to justify itself but to give the keenest possible shock of surprise at the end, one has only to recall that amazing bit of irony by Anatole France, *La Procurateur de Judee,* in which Pontius Pilate is talking in his old age with another Roman, indulging in reminiscences of his long-ago governorship in Palestine. Gradually, the friend brings up one memory after another, drawing closer and closer to the crowning event that has stamped itself upon his brain, the Crucifixion. Then comes the ironic surprise that gives the story its peculiar twist. Pontius Pilate shakes his head. "I don't remember," he says slowly. "But then, there were so many cases brought before me in those years!"

Chapter 5

# The Gospel of Infinite Pains

It was the Roman poet, Ovid, who once said, at least in substance, "It is a fact that some authors cannot correct. They compose with pleasure and with ardour; but they exhaust all their force. They fly with but one wing, when they revise their work; the first fire does not return."[1]

What was true in Ovid's day has been equally true in all periods of literary production. There are always certain authors, eminently brilliant some of them, who not only cannot revise, but rather pride themselves on their inability to do so. Byron, for instance, is a striking case in point. He is said to have written with astonishing rapidity—*The Corsair* in ten days, *The Bride of Abydos* in four days; while it was printing he added and corrected, but without recasting. To quote his own words:

> I told you before that I can never recast anything. I am like the tiger. If I miss the first spring, I go grumbling back to my jungle again; but if I do it, it is crushing.

Now, the ability to get one's thoughts upon paper with great rapidity is in itself an admirable gift. There is a freshness, a spontaneity, and oftentimes a crude strength in the first rough draft which must inevitably be partly sacrificed in the process of final polishing. There is a great deal of truth in Thoreau's advice:

---

1. Quoted in this form by Disraeli, *Curiosities of Literature,* who goes on to cite numerous interesting cases of industrious revision.

Write while the heat is in you. When the farmer burns a hole in his yoke, he carries the iron quickly from the fire to the wood, for every moment it is less effectual to penetrate it. . . . The writer who postpones the recording of his thoughts uses an iron which has cooled to burn a hole with. He cannot influence the minds of his audience.

"Write while the heat is in you" is, so far as it goes, excellent advice. Pages written under great heat and pressure are not unlikely to turn out diamonds in the rough—for this is Nature's way of making diamonds. The trouble with the advice is that it does not go half far enough; it tells only half the truth; it fails to point out that all the fire in the world will never do the effective finishing, or add the final lustre, like a little slow and patient rubbing, after the ideas have grown cold. In other words, one of the most fatal mistakes a young writer can make is in thinking that writing is just a matter of inspiration; that you either have the inborn talent, or you have not; that if you have it, you need only to plunge into a sort of vortex of creative energy, a fine sibylline frenzy—and your inborn talent will do the rest. That, of course, is arrant nonsense, and very disastrous nonsense, as well—because, if you once get the idea firmly fixed in your mind that a masterpiece can spring, like Pallas Athene, perfected from its author's brain, then good-bye to all hope for that honest drudgery, that loving patience over infinite detail, which is such an essential accompaniment of the creative gift that it almost justifies that threadbare paradox that genius is the art of taking infinite pains.

Now this, of course, is precisely what genius is not, and never can be, in literature any more than in the other arts. No amount of patient juggling with the contents of unabridged dictionaries will give birth to a great poem, if there is not the inspiration of a great thought back of it. The statement that if, according to the law of permutations, you toss a sufficient number of Greek alphabets up in the air, and keep on doing so for a sufficient number of times, they will sooner or later come down arranged to form the text of the *Iliad,* may be all right in higher mathematics, but it is not helpful to the Craftsmanship of Writing. But just because technique will not produce immortal epics all by itself, there is no sense in leaping to the other extreme, and either shirking it or discarding it altogether. The best laid stone-ballast railway track in the world won't take us anywhere unless we run trains upon it, but that is no reason for expecting our little intellectual railway trains to run themselves without any guide rails at all. Undisciplined genius is an erratic, irresponsible thing that people may admire on occasion, but dare not trust, for they never know what it is likely to do next. As between two artists of equal inborn talent a wise man would every time give preference to the one who, in addition to his inborn talent, shows the best command of that technical part of craftsmanship which comes only from persistent drilling. This, I take it, is the real point of that almost threadbare story of how Pope Benedict IX., wishing to have some paintings executed in St. Peter's, and having heard of the fame of the Florentine, Giotto, sent for some specimen or design by which he might judge Giotto's work; and how Giotto, with a turn of his hand, made a perfectly symmetrical circle and delivered it to the messenger, saying, "This is my design." This perfect circle was no evidence of an inborn talent, for nature does not endow any one of us at birth with the power of making perfect circles—whatever she may do for spiders in regard to equilateral polygons. But it was evidence of a trained hand, a perfect technique; and that is a pretty important matter to be assured of if you are ordering work done by a genius, whether you happen to be Pope Benedict IX. or anybody else.

The whole point of this illustration of Giotto's circle is, not merely that it is something which has to be learned, but that the learning costs an infinitude of practice. It is apparently such a simple thing to do and yet you can keep on trying and trying, day after day, month after month; and probably never in the whole course of your life reach the point where you won't have to say, "Yes, that is pretty good, but I ought to do better." That is precisely the feeling that a conscientious craftsman ought to have in regard to his writing. He may or may not be satisfied with the inspiration behind his work. For that, there is no rule; it depends upon the individual case. But in regard to the technical side, it would be well if he could always feel that it would be possible to do it just a little bit better—always feel that there is some one perfect way of building the structure or rounding the sentence that elusively keeps just beyond his reach.

Consequently, one of the first ideas that every young writer should promptly get into his head is that, whatever degree of talent he may have, there is no escape from a certain amount of tedious drudgery, if he ever expects to accomplish anything of real importance. It does not follow that the man who frankly says that he cannot revise his work after it is once written is necessarily in the second grade of authorship, any more than the man. who admits that he cannot map out his whole work in all its details before writing his opening sentence. There is no hard and fast rule as to the point at which the real drudgery of writing shall begin. Some authors have served their time in the ranks, as it were, before their first book has ever seen print; they have learned their craft pretty thoroughly by a thousand abortive efforts that have either never been set down on paper at all or else have gone speedily into the scrap-basket or the furnace fire. This does not mean that they will be relieved of the necessity of pruning and polishing; but it does mean that a long and faithful apprenticeship reduces the amount of such detail work to a minimum. Then again some writers have the trick of doing most of their verbal sand-papering in advance, turning and twisting each sentence a thousand times in their brain, before ever committing it to paper. That, when we stop to think of it, is the original, the natural way in which literary composition was evolved. The primitive sagas, the early folk tales were all slowly crystallised into shape, not only before they were reduced to writing, but before there was any writing into which to reduce them.

But it makes no difference at what point an author gets in his really hard work; there can be no definite rules laid down for preparation or for revision. There is no magic in a second re-writing or a third, in a fifth or a tenth revised proof. If the first draft of your sentence satisfies you, a second writing is a waste of time. But fifty re-writings are none too much if the forty-ninth still fails to content you. Every writer must in this respect work out his own particular method. A few years ago the statement went the rounds of the literary columns that Mr. Maurice Hewlett made a practice of re-writing all of his stories no less than four times; that each of these drafts was made with all the care that he could bestow upon it and when finished promptly destroyed; that the second would contain only so much of the first and the third only so much of the second as, by its excellence or its striking and peculiar phrasing, stamped itself upon his memory. Whether or not he really works in that way, such a method would, of course, account for many of Mr. Hewlett's peculiarities of style. But it might prove extremely disastrous to another author.

Some writers apply the Gospel of Infinite Pains from the first moment of their conception of a plot down to the last revision of the page proofs. Balzac was one of these. His erratic and laboured methods of revision, as recorded by Theophile Gautier in his *Portraits Contemporains,* are such an interesting object lesson of the extent to which the fever for revision may be carried that it seems worth while to quote him here rather extensively:

> His method of proceeding was as follows: When he had long borne and lived a subject, he wrote, in a rapid, uneven, blotted, almost hieroglyphic writing, a species of outline on several pages. These pages went to the printing office, from which they were returned in placards, that is to say, in detached columns in the centre of large sheets. He read these proofs attentively, for they already gave to his embryo work that impersonal character which manuscript never possesses; and he applied to this first sketch the great critical faculty with which he was gifted, precisely as though he were judging of another man's work.
>
> Then he began operations: approving or disapproving, he maintained or corrected, but above all he *added.* . . . After some hours, the paper might have been taken for a drawing of fireworks by a child. Rockets, darting from the original text, exploded on all sides. Then there were crosses: simple crosses, crosses re-crossed, like those of a blazon, stars, suns, Arabic figures, letters, Greek, Roman or French, all imaginable signs, mingled with erasures. Strips of paper, fastened on by wafers or pins, were added to the insufficient margins, and were rayed with lines of writing, very fine to save room, and full themselves of erasures; for a correction was hardly made before that again was corrected. . . .
>
> The following day, the proofs came back . . . the bulk of course doubled. Balzac set to work again, always amplifying . . . Often

this tremendous labour ended with an intensity of attention, a clearness of perception of which he alone was capable. He would see that the thought was warped by the execution, that an episode predominated; that a figure which he meant should be secondary for the general effect was projecting out of its plan. Then, with one stroke of his pen, he bravely annihilated the result of four or five nights of labour. He was heroic at such times.

Balzac, of course, was one of the colossals, and all of his methods, whether right or wrong, were colossal like himself. The vast majority of us will never write a *Comedie Humaine* nor overspread our proof sheets with mad pyrotechnics of erasures. Nevertheless, the essence of Balzac's method is a sound one. You can follow no better plan, provided your mind works that way, than to get your whole initial thought down on paper in the first heat of creation; and then, after a day or two, re-write and amplify, and re-write and amplify again, building up, little by little, filling in the details, smoothing the rough places until your work finally reaches a stage that you are content to keep as its permanent form. Yet even then, if you are a convert to the Gospel of Infinite Pains, you will still find some changes to make in your proof sheets, some further amendment to work into your second and third editions.

But, of course, it is possible to carry anything too far, even such an apparently limitless thing as Infinite Pains. Flaubert was the signal instance of this. His pursuit of perfection verged upon mania; his tireless zeal in connection with every detail of whatever work he had on hand for the moment was in the nature of a fixed idea. Zola, in his *Romanciers Naturalistes,* has given an admirably detailed account of Flaubert's methods of work in pursuit of "that perfection which made up the joy and the torment of his existence." When he had once got a rough draft upon paper the "chase after documents" began with as much method as possible:

He read above all a considerable number of works; or rather one should say that he merely skimmed them, going with an instinct of which he was rather proud, to the one page, the one phrase that would be of use to him. Often a work of five hundred pages would give him only a single note which he painstakingly transcribed; often also such a volume would give him nothing at all. Here we find an explanation of the seven years which he spent on an average on each one of his books; for he lost at least four in his preparatory readings.

And as he read, his notes piled up, overflowed his portfolios, became unwieldy, mountainous. To give some idea of his conscientiousness in gathering material, Zola mentions that before writing *L'Education Sentimentale* he ran through the entire collection of *Charivari,* in order to saturate himself with the spirit of petty journalism, under Louis-Philippe; and that it was out of the words found in that collection that he created the character of Hussonnet. At last an hour would come when, as Flaubert put it, he would feel the "need of writing":

> When he began the work of composition he would first write quite rapidly a piece consisting of a whole episode, five or six pages at most. Sometimes, when the right word would not come, he would leave it blank. Then he would start in again with this same piece, and it would be a matter of two or three weeks, sometimes more, of impassioned labour over those five or six pages. He wanted them perfect, and I assure you that perfection to him was not a simple matter. He weighed each word, examining not only the meaning but the conformation as well. Avoidance of repetitions, of rhymes, of harsh sounds was merely the rough beginning of his task. He went so far as not to allow the same syllables to recur in a phrase; sometimes a single letter got on his nerves and he would search for words in which it did not occur; then again he sometimes had need of a definite number of r's to give a rolling effect to a sentence.

All this is given here not as an example to be imitated by the young literary craftsman but as a sort of ultimate standard by which to measure the extent and the earnestness of his own efforts. Your latest story, perhaps, came back this morning accompanied by its third rejection slip. In writing that story did you take the trouble to work it over for the third or fourth time? Did you erase and rearrange the opening sentence endlessly until you knew all its possible variations by heart? Did you wake up suddenly in the night with a happy idea that would just fit into page seventeen and could not wait till morning?—or did you on the other hand, simply sit down quite comfortably one day, possessed only of pen, ink and paper and a good working idea, and dash off your five thousand words at top speed while the heat that Thoreau speaks of was still in you? And, as you signed your name, did you say to your. self, "Well, I suppose some of this is a bit ragged, but it will have to go as it is "? If the second is the case, then your collection of rejection slips deserves to multiply. You may be a genius, but you are not a craftsman. Better a hundred times the exaggeration, the hair-splittings, the *reductio ad absurdum* of Flaubert's Infinite Pains than such deliberate slovenliness. If you think that your lot is a hard one and that literature at best is a steady grind with slow results, read just one more paragraph on Flaubert's method and perhaps you will readjust your ideas.

One Sunday morning (writes Zola) we found him drowsy, broken with fatigue. The day before, in the afternoon, he had finished a page of Bouvard et Pecuchet, with which he felt very much pleased and he had gone to dine in town, after having copied it out on a large sheet of Holland paper that he was accustomed to use. When he returned about midnight, instead of retiring at once, he had to give himself the pleasure of rereading that page. But he became greatly disturbed, discovering that he had repeated himself within a space of two lines. Although there was no fire in his study and it was very cold, he obstinately set to work to get rid of that repetition. Then, finding other words which displeased him, he gave up the attempt to change them all and went to bed in despair. But once in bed, it was impossible to sleep; he turned and turned again, thinking always of those devils of words. All at once he hit upon a happy correction, sprang to the floor, relighted his candle and returned in his night-shirt to his study to write out the new phrase. After that he crawled back, shivering beneath the coverlets. Three times, he sprang up and re-lighted his candle, in order to change the position of a word or to alter a comma. At last, in desperation, dominated by the demon of perfection, he took his page with him, bundled his muffler around his ears, tucked himself in on all sides in his bed and until daybreak cut and pruned his page, covering it all over with pencil strokes. That was the way Flaubert worked. We all have manias of this sort, but with him it was this sort of mania from one end of his books to the other.

It is somewhat of a comfort to turn from a writer whose efforts were so vastly in excess of the bulk of his actual production and take up another novelist who holds a fairly eminent position in English literature and who, through long years of remarkable average fertility, succeeded in making the quality of his writing keep steady pace with the quantity—Anthony Trollope. His advice to young writers is not only interesting but valuable, provided it be taken understandingly. It has seemed worth while to quote from him rather often in these pages. Here is still another passage that is apropos:

> *Nulla dies sine linea.* Let that be their motto. And let their work be to them as is his common work to the common labourer. No gigantic efforts will then be necessary. He need tie no wet towels round his brow, nor sit for thirty hours at his desk without moving—as men have sat, or said that they have sat. More than nine-tenths of my literary work has been done in the last twenty years, and during twelve of those years I followed another profession. I have never been a slave to this work, giving due time, if not more than due time, to the amusements I have loved. But I have been constant—and constancy in labour will conquer all difficulties. *Curia carat lapidem non vi, sed saepe cadendo.*

Steady, plodding work: that is Trollope's panacea for success in literature. "Let their work be to them as is his work to the common labourer," that is the one phrase to be treasured up and committed to memory. The art of writing—that is the part that savours of genius, the part for which we cannot prescribe rules, the part which makes laws unto itself. But the craftsmanship is a different matter. It may be congenial labour, but labour it must always be, differing in kind but not in degree from that of the hewer of wood or the tiller of the field. The great thing is to make it honest labour, to be quite sure that we are not skimping it or doing it grudgingly. We must each of us find our .own best working hours, must decide for ourselves whether we will sit thirty hours at a stretch without moving, and then do nothing more for a week, or whether we will accept the monotony of systematic daily effort from breakfast until luncheon, day in and day out, whether we feel like it or not. Some men can work that way, and some men cannot: and that is all there is about it; they cannot tell you why, they simply find that that is their individual case. Now, there is no virtue in one way more than in another—but whatever method of work you follow remember always that there is no such thing as a royal road to literary achievement, that it always means sooner or later work, work of the hardest, most earnest sort, and often the hardest of all work where it shows the least. For the greatest triumph of writing, as of other arts, is to conceal most carefully those spots upon which you have most conscientiously practised the Gospel of Infinite Pains.

Chapter 6

# The Question of Clearness

WE have seen in an earlier chapter that the first step towards good craftsmanship is to have a clear underlying purpose, and also that the resulting written work will be judged largely in accordance with the degree of nearness that it has attained in carrying that purpose out. But it is necessary to remember always that your book will be judged not according to the purpose as you have formulated it somewhere in the background of your own brain, but as you have expressed it in your written words. There is small use in having any underlying purpose at all until you have learned how to convey your meaning to others—in other words, until you have learned the paramount importance of clearness.

Clearness is so inseparable an element of all good writing that many a critic and rhetorician has regarded it as a term almost synonymous with that illusive quality called style. Professor A. S. Hill, for instance, who for so many years occupied the chair of English at Harvard University, chose to divide style under three heads: to the intellectual quality of style he gave the name, "Clearness;" to the emotional, "Force;" and to the esthetic, "Elegance." And many another teacher of rhetoric has similarly invented his own special classification and definition. But according to the ordinary and common sense understanding of the terms, clearness is not so much an element of style as it is a condition precedent to it, just as health is not beauty, but a condition precedent to beauty. Clearness may be that crystal transparency of word and phrase that belongs to finished art, or it may be the mere dry bones of fact picked clean of the last shred and fragment of adornment. For example, a washing list or a recipe for making Dill pickles may be perfectly clear, but there is a manifest absurdity in speaking of either as possessing style. But whether the dividing line between clearness and style is vague or sharply defined, there can be no question that if one must choose between the two evils it is far better to sacrifice the second of these qualities than the first. The writer who has said something definite and intelligible has achieved a tangible result even though he may have said it very badly; but the writer whose meaning is obscure has accomplished nothing at all, however well balanced and harmonious his phrases may sound. It is well to remember that the true function of words, like that of all building materials, is to be useful first and ornamental afterwards; and that for the greater part of what we have to say the simplest phrasing is the best, just as the really well dressed man is he whose clothes possess that quiet refinement which does not obtrude. But a scorn of flamboyant neckties and checkerboard trousers is no excuse for going to the opposite extreme of a blue flannel shirt and overalls; and when Stendhal in his intolerance of over elaboration and rhetorical flourish boasted that he formed his own style by daily readings of the Civil Code, he erred as badly on his side as the models he avoided erred on theirs. The best evidence that you are in sound bodily health is that it does not occur to you to think about it; and similarly a healthy literary style is that which does nothing overtly to direct our attention to it.

Now it seems as though the quality of clearness ought to need no definition; as though anyone possessed of normal understanding ought to grasp the fact that it simply denotes the ability to express in words any particular thought that you may have shaped in your mind and to express it in such succinct and unmistakable terms that any reader of ordinary intelligence will receive in his own brain a faithful image of that thought and be able at request to mirror it faithfully back to you in his own words. Yet, as a matter of fact, clearness is a quality that is either very much misunderstood or else quite wantonly disregarded. There are a large number of writers, and able writers too, who seem to think that they are quite clear enough if they get their thoughts down in a form capable of being understood by the reader who goes to work to extract the meaning with something of that energy with which one applies the nut-cracker to a refractory nut. This whole question of clearness has been so admirably discussed by Anthony Trollope in his *Autobiography* that I cannot do a greater service to young writers than by quoting it in its entirety:

> Any writer who has read even a little will know what is meant by the word intelligible. It is not sufficient that there be a meaning that may be hammered out of the sentence, but that the language should be so pellucid that the meaning should be rendered without an effort of the reader;—and not only some proposition of meaning, but the very sense, no more and no less, which the writer has intended to put into his words. What Macaulay says should be remembered by all writers: "How little the all-important art of making meaning pellucid is studied now! Hardly any popular author except myself thinks of it." The language used should be as ready and as efficient a conductor of the mind of the writer to the mind of the reader as the electric spark which passes from one battery to another battery. In all written matter the spark should carry everything; but in matters recondite the recipient will search to see that he misses nothing, and that he takes nothing away too much. The novelist cannot expect that any such search will be made. A young writer, who will acknowledge the truth of what I am saying, will often feel himself tempted by the difficulties of language to tell himself that some one little doubtful passage, some single collocation of words, which is not quite what it ought to be, will not matter. I know well what a stumbling-block such a passage may be. But he should leave nothing behind him as he goes on. The habit of writing clearly soon comes to the writer who is a severe critic to himself.

As a broad generalization, the concluding words of the above passage may be accepted as true enough in the case of the writer who has learned self-criticism and whose fault lies simply in a careless or slovenly use of English. But unfortunately there are many kinds and grades of obscurity ranging all the way from the obscurity of ignorance and stupidity to the obscurity that comes of too much learning and of hair-splitting analysis—all the way from an inability to think clearly down to an erudition with which the reader cannot keep pace. There is nothing to be gained by classifying and distinguishing, after the fashion of a school rhetoric, the various kinds of obscurity that it is possible to find in literature—by dividing what is ambiguous from what is vague and again what is vague from what is really obscure; because, while it is possible to make such a classification to almost any degree of minuteness that you choose, all these different kinds of verbal turbidness go back to one or more of the four primal causes that stand in the way of clearness; and the important thing is to get these four causes definitely in our minds,

The simplest way in which to approach the whole question is to recognize that when we write a book or a magazine article we are under a sort of implied contract to the class of readers whom we are trying to reach—that we have pledged ourselves to tell them something which we assume that they want to know. Now, in order to fulfil this obligation, we must bring about what the legal fraternity are fond of speaking of as "a meeting of minds,"—and of course there can be no meeting of minds unless we have learned to write intelligibly. There is no implied contract to write with any specified degree of form and elegance, any more than there is any agreement on the part of the express company which delivers the book or magazine to bring it in an automobile or a coach-and-four. The express company simply agrees to deliver the goods; and when we write, we agree, first of all, to deliver the ideas, and if we are obscure we have not delivered them.

Now in order that the minds of author and reader shall meet, there are four conditions requisite: first, that the author shall know what he is trying to say; second, that he shall be able to say it in the simplest terms; third, that his language shall be adapted to the requirement of his readers; fourth, that his thoughts shall not be beyond their range of comprehension. Perhaps you have been criticised for your want of clearness and you come to me for help. The first thing to find out is which of the above four requisites is your stumbling-block. Of course, if the trouble comes from the first, an inability to think clearly; if your thoughts are a muddle, if you are too lazy to straighten them out, there is no use in talking to you about how to write clearly. There is no use in expecting clearness from a slough; and the more accurately you succeed in mirroring back your own mental attitude the more hopelessly turbid what you write is bound to be. The first thing to do is to try to guide your thoughts into a straight channel and get them gradually into the habit of flowing deep and clear—somewhat after the fashion that marshlands are redeemed by a system of irrigation ditches. Your trouble may be simply inexperience, or laziness; or again it may be a constitutional inability to think logically, a fundamental lack of one vital element of the inborn talent.

But let us assume that you have learned to think clearly. The next step is to learn to write as clearly as you think. If your stumbling-block lies at this point, there is hope for you. If you know what you want to say and yet manage to tangle up your thoughts in a snarl of words, that is sheer bad writing and there is no excuse for it. No one who can think straight has any business to write badly. There is no necessity for it, because it is the easiest of all errors for which to obtain outside help. It is a simple question of fact whether a given paragraph does or does not convey the meaning you want it to when read by the casual reader of average intelligence. It is not a matter of expert judgment; it involves no canon of art any more than the question whether a landscape painter's picture of a Holstein cow looks like a cow or a black and white sign-post. If a country-bred child, looking at that cow, calls it a sign-post, all the art critics in the world cannot free that painter from the reproach of obscurity. So, if you are in doubt whether or not you write clearly you need not apply to a professional critic. You can always find someone near at hand to help you, some patient, long-suffering member of your immediate family circle, and preferably someone who is not literary—someone who more nearly represents the so-called "general public." Read your paragraphs to him and then ask him, "What does this mean to you? What have I tried to say? "If your amateur critic is dubious, if he arrives at a wrong idea, or catches the right one only after an obvious effort, then what you have written is badly done and must be written over. Now of course he cannot tell you just why it is badly done, or what particular words and phrases are misleading, or what would be the simplest twist by which to remedy them. He simply throws the burden back on you where it belongs; you will have to grope for the remedy; and a little groping, a little more hard work will not hurt you. What your friend has done is simply to serve a purpose analogous to that of re-translation in the case of documents such as patent-right papers or international treaties, where the first translator turns the original from English into French, and a second translator reconverts it into English—and if the last version differs from the original, the translation must be all done over.

But besides the practical method of experimenting with your writings on your friends, there are a few simple principles to keep in mind that will often save you from stumbling. Do not let rules of rhetoric and style stand in the way of clearness; cheerfully break any one of them rather than be obscure. It may be villainously bad style to allow the same word to recur half a dozen times upon a page; but it would be better to repeat that word half a dozen times within a single line rather than to lack clearness. Professor Barrett Wendell offers a case in point when he writes:

> Clearness I may best define as the distinguishing quality of a style that cannot be misunderstood. To be thoroughly clear, it is not enough that style express the writer's meaning; style must so express this meaning that no rational reader can have any doubt as to what the meaning is. To come as near clearness as I could, for example, I deliberately avoided pronouns in that last sentence, repeating style and meaning with a clumsiness defensible only on the score of lucidity.

And Macaulay, discussing the use of the French word, *abbe,* in place of the English, *abbot,* expresses the same rule even more forcibly:

> We do not like to see French words introduced into English composition: but, after all, the first law of writing, that law to which all other laws are subordinate, is this, that the words employed shall be such as convey to the reader the meaning of the writer. Now an abbot is the head of a religious house; an abbe is quite a different sort of person. It is better undoubtedly

to use an English word than a French word; but it is better to use a French word than to misuse an English word.

And in this connection we must not forget the words of the genial *Autocrat of the Breakfast Table:* "The divinity student looked as if he would like to question my Latin. No sir, I said—you need not trouble yourself. There is a higher law in grammar not to be put down by Andrew and Stoddard."

If you would be clear cultivate simplicity and brevity. But remember that brevity is not always synonymous with the smallest possible number of words. As Edgar Allan Poe once wisely wrote: "The most truly concise style is that which most rapidly transmits the sense. . . . Those are mad who admire brevity which squanders our time for the purpose of economizing our printing-ink and paper." Never hesitate to use as many words as are required to convey your meaning, your whole meaning and nothing but your meaning, beyond the shadow of a doubt. A rather good way to acquire a simple style is to try to write more in the manner of ordinary conversation. And the reason for this may be readily understood by analogy with a simple rule for fencing, laid down in one of Marion Crawford's Italian novels, by his memorable duelist, the melancholy Spicca. We are accustomed, Spicca explained, from early childhood, to point at things with our index finger; indeed, through immemorial generations it has become a sort of inborn instinct. We have no need to close one eye and carefully sight along the finger: we point with an accuracy that is almost incredible. But it does not come naturally to us to point with a stick or a sword; and that is why Spicca acquired his wonderful dexterity by simply laying his index finger along the blade of his weapon and pointing with that. In like manner, we have all been accustomed from childhood to point, as it were, with spoken words; and this we do with a fair degree of accuracy, for otherwise we should frequently fail to obtain what we want. But we have not been accustomed from childhood to point with written words; so it is at least an experiment worth trying to lay the index finger of ordinary conversation along the written line and see if this does not improve the accuracy of our aim.

Some reader is almost certain to raise the objection that the result of such an experiment will be an excess of colloquialism. But there is no foundation for any such fear. It would be impossible by any means short of a phonograph to emulate the carelessness, the redundancy, the elisions and slurrings of even rather careful conversation. In fiction where a trained and observant author deliberately tries his best to make the conversation of his characters quite like that of real life, he almost invariably errs on the side of artificiality, always makes them speak a little more carefully than they really do. And what holds true of conversation of course applies with double strength to narrative description or critical analysis. But the effect of the collo-quial tone while never quite reaching the level of actual conversation does tend to make the general tone of serious reading lighter and more inviting. "The writing," says Miss Edgeworth, "which has least the appearance of literary manufacture almost always pleases me the best;" while St. Beuve is still more outspoken: "To accustom oneself," he says, "to write as one speaks and as one thinks, is that not already a long step towards accustoming oneself to think wisely? "

One method which I personally have found to work well, both in my own case and in that of other writers of my acquaintance, is to thresh out a difficult episode or problem in conversation, talking the whole thing over, sometimes with several people in succession, and thus gradually clarifying the underlying thought and crystallising the form of its expression. It often happens that some phrase or expression which has baffled and eluded us for days in the privacy of our study suddenly flashes into definite shape in the heat of a discussion; or the one tantalising word that a phrase lacked to clinch the meaning beyond question leaps to the tip of the speaker's tongue when it had persistently refused to come at the call of the pen. And after all is not this a perfectly natural and easily understood conse-quence of the way in which the whole art of literary composition must have developed? Authorship antedates by unmeasured centuries the discovery of letters and the art of writing. The inherited habit of composition in the form of oral verse and prose is vastly older than our modern practice of secluding ourselves and scratching down rows of little black symbols on a white expanse of paper, or still more incongruously tapping celluloid keys with the tips of our fingers. The whole advantage of the conversational method, however, has nowhere been more delightfully expressed than by Oliver Wendell Holmes, through the lips of the Autocrat:

I rough out my thoughts in talk, as an artist models in clay. Spoken language is so plastic—you can pat or coax, and spread and shave, and rub out and fill up, and stick on so easily, when you work that soft material, that there is nothing like it for modeling. Out of it come the shapes which you turn into marble or bronze in your immortal books, if you happen to write such.

But it does no good to think and to write clearly, unless you write in a language intelligible to the class of readers whom you are trying to reach. The most crystalline prose of the clearest French thinkers remains meaningless to the reader possessed of only a smattering of Ollendorf. As our familiarity with a foreign tongue progresses, the very last stage of proficiency is that complete and instantaneous comprehension, as the eye glances down the printed page, with no sense of effort, no consciousness of an intervening veil. In a minor degree, we all know how irksome even a very clever dialect story may become; the page is studded over with words and phrases that convey, first of all, a sense of strangeness. An account of a horse-race or a prize-fight, in the sporting columns of our daily papers may be admirably lucid to the readers for whom it is intended; but to many of us it speaks in an unknown tongue.

Professor Barrett Wendell, in his chapter on Clearness, already referred to, gives a rather amusing example drawn from football parlance. Centre-rush and half-back, and a score of similar words, he admits, are regularly constructed compounds formed from perfectly familiar English words and yet to him devoid of any definite meaning. But, he goes on to say, he has been informed and he believes that there are students in his own lecture courses to whom these same words have a real significance. Similarly, a treatise on some special branch of physics or botany or civil engineering may be couched in the clearest possible terms and yet convey no meaning at all to the reader unversed in those sciences. For instance, I open quite at random the fourth volume of a recent *Reference Handbook of the Medical Science* and I learn:

Double hemiplegia is synonymous with cerebral paraplegia, both indicating a paraplegia of intracranial origin, involving the cerebral motor-tracts. A peripheral paraplegia may be produced by a multiple neuritis involving the peripheral nerves of both lower extremities in such a symmetrical manner as closely to resemble spinal-cord lesions.

I am quite prepared to believe that there is nothing intricate in the thought that lies concealed behind this barrier of technical vocabulary; I simply realise that I am not one of tile readers for whom it was intended. But for me it might just as well be the "washing list in Babylonian cuneiform "of which we are told by Gilbert and Sullivan's Modern Major General.

If you are writing upon a technical subject for a special public, you must use a special vocabulary. If you are the sporting editor on a daily paper, you must write of football in football jargon; but on the other hand, if you are discussing the educational value of football in a pedagogical magazine, you will use a different and simpler terminology. And in each case what you write may be quite clear to the audience for whom you intend it. The only thing to guard against is the chance of making a mistake in your audience, the danger of attributing to them a special knowledge which they do not possess. For that reason, it is a good plan to underrate rather than overrate the average intelligence of your readers. Any physician can understand what has happened if you say that a man has broken the bones of his forearm, but readers who are not physicians may have to stop and think if you write that he has suffered a fracture of both radius and ulna.

And in the fourth place, your vocabulary may be of the simplest and yet your work may convey to a large majority of readers a sense of inpenetrable density. There are, for instance, some branches of higher mathematics in which a person with a fair average knowledge of algebra and geometry will encounter no terms or symbols that are strange to his eye; and yet the meaning of what he reads will leave his mind absolutely blank. The difficulty in this case lies outside of any question of craftsmanship; it is inherent in the subject matter itself. When you come across a book or article of this type you have to recognize that it is not intended for you, or at least that you are not yet ripe for it. The novels of Mr. Henry James are one of the best possible instances of. this type of book. Mr. James has mannerisms, many of them; he has a curious, and to some readers an exasperatingly confusing way of introducing all his modifiers, his provisos and saving clauses parenthetically before reaching the conclusion of his main sentence. But all of these things put together would not account for the difficulty that many people find in reading Henry James. The real secret of his obscurity lies much deeper. It is because he is attempting to pursue his analysis of the human heart and soul to an unattainable point; to differentiate motives with a hairsplitting minuteness. His books are a form of experimental psychology too intricate and erudite ever to be expressed with perfect clearness. And when we encounter this sort of obscurity we must recognise that it is something which is inherent in the subject matter itself; in other words, that the book is one of limited appeal to a specially chosen audience.

Chapter 7

# The Question of Style

There is, I think, a good deal of unnecessary heartburn experienced by young writers regarding the question whether or not they are beginning to form a style. It indicates a hypochondriacal condition of mind akin to the familiar tendency of so many young medical students to believe that they are suffering from various purely imaginary diseases. A sound mind in a sound body is too busy in performing the numerous activities belonging to each day's work to stop to count the heart-beats or the rate of respiration. Any young writer, possessed of something really worth saying, and a certain driving energy that makes him bent upon saying it in the clearest and most forceful way that he possibly can, ought to be too intent upon the task at hand to be worrying about whether he is forming a style—whether, in other words, his brave beginnings of today are cornerstones in the arch of future fame.

Style is the aroma of literature, comparable to the bouquet of old wine. You cannot age a new vintage over night by any artificial process. No writer, by taking thought, can add a cubit to his height as a stylist. It is a matter of growth, and slow ripening. We have seen that what every young writer should first strive to acquire is a clear-cut idea of what he is trying to accomplish; that, secondly, he should aim at a technical skill which will enable him to build the framework of his creations, whatever their form may be, solidly and according to the proportions demanded by good art; and thirdly, that he must cultivate that infinite patience which will strive to make all parts and all aspects of his work tend toward a unity of effect in subject and structure and language. And when a writer has learned thoroughly to do these things, he need no longer worry about style, for style is nothing else than the ability to express one's thoughts in the best possible way. "Style," says James Russell Lowell, "is the establishment of a perfect mutual understanding between the worker and his material." And Walter Pater expresses very nearly the same thought in somewhat different terms when he writes:

> To give the phrase, the sentence, the structural member, the entire composition, song or essay, a similar unity with its subject and with itself:—style is in the right way when it tends toward that.

The ability to express one's thoughts in the best possible way—that is a rather bigger contract than at first appears. Not merely to express one's thoughts in the clearest possible way, or the most forcible, or the most florid, or the most faultlessly grammatical way. It means a great deal more than any one of these, or all of them taken together. It means the nicest possible compromise between clearness, let us say, on the one hand, and metaphor on the other; or between the realism of speech, and the dignity of narrative verse; or between the special effects of contrast and a general effect of uniformity. In its widest definition, there is nothing that can be said or written in any language under the sun that has not its special ideal of style—some one form most appropriate to it: and to some degree the ability to attain approximately this desired norm is an element of the Inborn Talent;—just as marksmanship of any kind is partly a matter of practice and partly also a matter of natural aptitude.

If you examine in succession a series of definitions of style, taken at random from various authorities, you will find the divergence between them rather confusing. The more you read, the more confused you are likely to become. The trouble, of course, is a lack of agreement on the part of the authorities regarding the nature and extent of the quality which they are trying to define. One writer, for instance, assumes that style is a combination of clearness, force and elegance; another looks upon style as a blending of a certain abstract perfection of writing with the personal element, which at

best is manner and at worst is mannerism, while still a third considers style as something apart from the personal equation—a sort
of ideal goal towards which we press, but which we never attain.
The same discrepancy is noticeable in the use of the word, style,
in other connections—take it, for instance, in the matter of dress.
Now clearness of purpose in dress involves the intent of clothing the
body and keeping it warm; and in this elemental sense one hears
people speak of the style of clothes worn by peasants, or artisans,
or savage tribes. A certain proportion of people, on the other hand,
think of style in dress as a sort of self-advertisement, a matter of
force and emphasis, a question of flamboyance and the *dernier cri*.
And there are still others who, with a finer conservatism, understand
style to be that rare art in dress which *effects* a perfect compromise
between the prevailing fashion and the personality, and which un-
erringly chooses, in color and in form, the garment best designed
to suit, most completely and at the same time most unobtrusively
the individual need.

Now there is no logic in looking upon any one of these definitions
of style as being right and the rest of them all wrong. The one thing
needful to know is which view any particular critic holds, for then any
apparent contradiction disappears. I am inclined to think, however,
for the purpose of good craftsmanship, that the most helpful view to
hold is the third of those given above: namely, that style is an ideal
goal towards which we struggle, but forever unattainable. Try to
think of style in literature somewhat as you think of the copper-plate
line of Spencerian penmanship at the top of the page in a copy-
book—as the model towards which the pupil is faithfully striving,
but which it would be undesirable for him to attain with complete
fidelity. Without some such model to follow, no one ever acquires a
good handwriting; but, on the other hand, no one with any sort of
individuality wants to write like a copy-book. Think how character in
handwriting strengthens and deepens with the passing years—and it
will do this quite regardless of whether we started with a good or
bad model at the top of our page. But what a gulf there is between
the handwriting that is clear, and artistic and individual, and that
which has individuality and nothing else! And to a far greater extent
do we feel the difference between the writer who has style and
individuality, and him who has individuality without style.

My advice, then, to the beginner in writing is: do not worry too much about your style: do not be all the time counting your literary pulse. Try to write as simply and as clearly as you can and without self-consciousness. In learning the rudiments of your art you are like the novice in archery learning to hit a target. Concentrate yourself upon the task of making your verbal shafts reach their mark. If you do this faithfully, ease and grace should follow in their own due time.

Do not assume, however, that if you are faithful, you will acquire one of the few masterly styles in literature. It is given to the very few to attain this. Be satisfied if you succeed in keeping near enough to your copper-plate model so that your mannerisms will be overlooked, or if you succeed in say anything of such importance that your readers think more of what you say than how you say it. Wine, as said above, acquires bouquet only in the course of years; but no number of years can ever give bouquet to a poor vintage. Nevertheless a good many attempts have been made, and with some degree of apparent success, to age, a literary style. Certain writers have deliberately set themselves, as part of their apprenticeship, the task of practicing the mannerisms of a few recognized masters of English prose. Stevenson is a conspicuous example of this practice, and the quality of his prose is admittedly a result of such self-training. In his essay, "A College Magazine," he has himself outlined his method as follows:

> Whenever I read a book or a passage that particularly pleased me, in which a thing was said or an effect rendered with pro-priety, in which there was either some conspicuous force or some happy distinction in the style, I must sit down at once and set myself to ape that quality. . . . I thus played the sedulous ape to Hazlitt, to Lamb, to Wordsworth, to Sir Thomas Browne, to Defoe, to Hawthorne, to Montaigne, to Baudelaire, and to Obermann. . . . That, like it or not, is the way to learn to write.

Yet, where this method succeeds with one man out of ten, it is quite likely to do more harm than good to the nine others, making them mere copyists—like a young painter who spends his days reproducing a Raphael or a Rubens, instead of remaining under the open sky, learning to express his own thoughts in his own way. Some teachers, indeed, question whether any real benefit accrues from conscious imitation of another man's style. Professor A. S. Hill has put himself on record in the following emphatic manner:

> In a great writer the style is the man—the man as made by his ancestors, his education, his career, his circumstances, and his genius.
>
> It is idle, then, to attempt to secure a good style by imitating this or that writer; for the best part of a good style is incommunicable. An imitator may, if he applies himself closely to the task, catch mannerisms and reproduce defects, and perhaps superficial merits; but most valuable qualities, those that have their root in character, he will miss altogether, except in so far as his own personality resembles that of his model.

Of course, between these two extremes; the belief, on the one hand, that conscious imitation is the only way to learn to write; and on the other, that it is no way at all to learn, the truth, as usual lies somewhere midway. Yet it is worth noting that even Stevenson has not escaped reproach. Mr. H. D. Traill, for instance, complains that his style "suffers somewhat from its evidences of too conscious art"; Henry James says, in friendly criticism that his style "has nothing accidental or diffident; it is eminently conscious of its responsibilities and meets them with a kind of gallantry—as if language were a pretty woman, and a person who proposed to handle it had, of necessity, to be something of a Don Juan." And Professor Saintsbury is even more emphatic:

> Adopting to the full, and something more than the full, the modern doctrine of the all-importance of art, of manner, of style in literature, Mr. Stevenson early made the most elaborate studies in imitative composition. There is no doubt that he at last succeeded in acquiring a style which was quite his own; but it was complained, and with justice, that even to the last he never obtained complete ease in this style; its mannerism was not only excessive, but bore, as even excessive mannerism by no means always does, the marks of distinct and obvious effort.

Now it is quite likely that in reading Stevenson you are not conscious of this "distinct and obvious effort" of which Professor Saintsbury speaks; personally, I always am—although that does not prevent me from appreciating his worth in literature. But the fact strengthens me in the conviction that I am right in saying that to ask oneself continually, "Am I acquiring a style?" is apt to bring one little profit. It is like a novice in painting similarly asking, "Am I learning to mix colours?" A painter does not need to distress himself about the beauty and harmony of all the colours that he may sooner or later be called upon to mix—the important thing is to do the best he can to obtain the particular colour that he needs for the moment. "Colour is a gift," says Dick Heldar to Maisie, in *The Light that Failed,* "Put it aside and think no more about it." Similarly, although the parallel is not wholly true, a beginner will certainly do himself no great harm by assuming that in the craft of writing, style is a gift that may for the time be put aside and forgotten. Be sure that for the beginner the least style is the best style. Do not polish excessively; and when you do polish, be sure that you have something that is worthy of polishing. It is well to put a lustre on solid mahogany; but it is foolish to expend energy and good wax upon soft pine.

Of course, if you want to go somewhat deeply into the whole question, you might begin by reading what various recognised stylists have said upon the subject; you might make yourself familiar with De Quincey's *Essay on Style* and Pater's; and what Lowell has to say, and Stevenson too and half a dozen more besides to whom they will readily guide you. And the chances are that after a few hours, or days, of diligent reading you will come away with a considerable sense of discouragement and confusion; because, while they all fairly agree that style is a question of fitting the method to the material; and that there is not one style but there are many styles, just as there may be many forms of dress to suit different occupations; yet after all they do not lay down rules that are really helpful. Some comfort is to be gained out of Pater, if read understandingly, for he has a broad sanity of outlook that recognises merit in a great diversity of methods. Here, for instance, is a paragraph which embodies the essence of all he has to say on this subject and is well worth pondering upon:

In the highest, as in the lowest literature, the one indispensable beauty is, after all, truth:—truth to bare facts in the latter,
as to some personal sense of fact; diverted somewhat from
men's ordinary sense of it, in the former: truth there as accuracy,
truth here as expression, that finest and most intimate form
of truth, the *vraie verité*. And what an eclectic principle this
really is! Employing for its one sole purpose—that absolute
accordance of expression to idea—all other literary beauties
and excellencies whatever: how many kinds of style it covers,
explains, justifies and, at the same time, safeguards! Scott's
facility, Flaubert's deeply pondered evocation of "the phrase"
are equally good art. Say what you have to say, what you have
a will to say, in the simplest, the most direct and exact manner
possible, with no surplusage: there is the justification of the
sentence so fortunately born, "entire, smooth and round," that
it needs no punctuation, and also (that is the point!) of the most
elaborate period, if it be right in its elaboration. Here is the office
of ornament; here also the purpose of restraint in ornament.
. . . The seeming baldness of *Le Rouge et le Noir* is nothing in
itself; the wild ornament of *Les Misérables* is nothing in itself;
and the restraint of Flaubert, amid a real natural opulence,
only redoubled beauty—the phrase so large and so precise at
the same time, hard as bronze, in service to the more perfect
adaptation of words to their matter.

Literature, by finding its specific excellence in the absolute
correspondence of the term to. its import, will be but fulfilling
the condition of all artistic quality in things everywhere, of all
good art.

It is Pater who says of the author of *Madame Bovary,* "If all high
things have their martyrs, Gustave Flaubert might perhaps rank
as the martyr of literary style "; and in support of this opinion he
proceeds to quote the following summary of Flaubert's literary creed:

> Possessed of an absolute belief that there exists but one way
> of expressing one thing, one word to call it by, one adjective to
> qualify, one verb to animate it, he gave himself to superhuman

labour for the discovery, in every phrase, of that word, that verb, that epithet. In this way, he believed in some mysterious harmony of expression, and when a true word seemed to him to lack euphony, still went on seeking another, with invincible pains, certain that he had not yet got hold of the word. . . . A thousand preoccupations would beset him at the same moment, always with this desperate certitude fixed in his spirit: Amongst all the expressions in the world, all forms and turns of expression, there is but one—one form, one mode—to express what I want to say.

Now, theoretically Flaubert is right; there are no perfectly equivalent synonyms either of words or phrases—and even the same phrase will take on shades of meaning when spoken by different lips. Whenever you utter a sentence you have expressed a thought in the only way in which that particular thought down to the last hair-splitting shade of meaning can be expressed. Change a syllable and you change the meaning—that was Flaubert's doctrine and it meant torture to him. And the trouble, of course, was that he tried to practise what can never be more than theoretical. It would be a great comfort to believe, with Emerson, that "There is no choice of words for him who clearly sees the truth; that provides him with the best word"; but to most of us such clearness of vision is denied. If a writer could really know down to the ultimate shade of thought exactly what he wanted to say and exactly the tone in which he wanted to say it, and if his brain was so equipped that it had at command the entire contents of the unabridged dictionary then, theoretically, the one inevitable word-sequence ought forthwith to present itself to him. In practice, however, there are a hundred different ways that occur to us for saying even some quite simple thing, each of them not precisely what we want to say, but representing a compromise, a sacrifice, on the side of meaning, or of euphony, or of rhythm. The one perfect way is the dream of a visionary, a forever unattainable ideal. We may come more or less near to it in proportion to our ten talents or our two talents or our one, but it always eludes us. And the finer the artist, the more he is apt to suffer because he sees so clearly how far short he has fallen. Style, then, practically means the ability to choose the words that will give us just the right meaning, just the right harmony, just the right cadence. And if this is to be done worthily we must attain our results so far as possible without straying afield for queer, exotic words and phrases. It is, says Lowell, "the secondary intellect which asks for excitement in expression, and stimulates itself into mannerism, which is the wilful obtrusion of self, as style is its unconscious abnegation." And Maupassant, in his well-known preface to *Pierre et Jean,* wrote in similar strain:

> There is no need of the bizarre, complicated, extensive and Chinese vocabulary that they force upon us today under the name of artistic writing to catch all the shades of thought; but it is necessary to discern with extreme lucidity all the modifications in the value of a word according to the place it occupies. Let us have fewer nouns, verbs and adjectives with meanings almost incomprehensible, but let us have more different phrases.

In regard to vocabulary no better rule has been formulated down to the present day than that old dictum of Quintillian: "Use only the newest of the old and the oldest of the new." We may, of course, assume in theory that no word is so obsolete that it may not under some special conditions be revived; no slang so recent as to be wholly barred out of print. D'Annunzio, the recognised master of modern Italian style, has ransacked the early writers for so many out-of-the-way words that some of his later prose can be more easily read by a college bred Anglo-Saxon with a fair knowledge of the language than by an equally intelligent Italian who does not happen to be well grounded in Latin and Greek. And in the opposite scale, we have Mr. Kipling, who fearlessly enriches our language with such words as he thinks it needs. Nevertheless, the safe norm lies in the simple, every-day vocabulary. A good craftsman can accomplish wonderful things with a limited number of tools: a certain eminent surgeon has been known to perform successfully an operation for appendicitis with no other instrument than a simple pair of scissors. One trouble with many of us is that we overwork just a few words and combinations of words, and neglect other equally good combinations; we have the vice of the hackneyed phrase. A well-known American critic once said

in conversation that he would rather be caught stealing a watch than
saying that a book "filled a long-felt want "—and unquestionably the
two offences differ in kind rather than degree. It was Daudet who
expressed the philosophy of the hackneyed phrase perhaps rather
more felicitously than any other:

> What profound disgust must those epithets feel which have
> lived for centuries with the same nouns! Bad writers cannot be
> made to comprehend this. They think divorce is not permitted to
> words. There are people who write without blushing: *venerable
> trees, melodious accents. Venerable* is not an ugly word; put it with
> another substantive—"your venerable burden," "most venerable
> worth," etc.—you see the union is good. In short, the epithet
> should be the mistress of the substantive, never its lawful wife.
> Between words there must be passing liaisons, but no eternal
> marriages. It is that which distinguishes the original writer from
> others.

It is that, an Anglo-Saxon critic finds himself instinctively adding,
that distinguishes just a few of the more prominent British writers of the young school; writers otherwise very wide apart indeed—Rudyard Kipling and Maurice Hewlett, Joseph Conrad and
Alfred Ollivant and J. C. Snaith—to mention only a few striking
examples. Each of these has a style of his own; some of them, indeed,
have a number of styles, to be donned and doffed upon occasion; but
the one trait that they all have in common is a frank audacity of new
combinations, a tendency to take liberties with noun and adjective,
and pair them off with as little ceremony as a hostess pairs off her
guests for a cotillion—and with as little malice. De Quincey wrote,
not without a grain of literary snobbishness:

> Like boys who are throwing the sun's rays in the eyes of a
> mob by means of a mirror, you must shift your lights and vibrate
> your reflections at every possible angle, if you would agitate the
> popular mind extensively.

De Quincey, of course, had a certain ingrained scorn of the popular
mind. It was quite unconsciously, while here intending to stigmatise a

type of bad rhetoric, that he actually gave us a rather vivid metaphor of the principle upon which language tends constantly to renew itself.

And this brings us to a vital point in the whole question of acquiring style. If you are proposing to learn the craft of building, or pottery making, or carpet weaving, will you be satisfied to know nothing beyond what has been done by England or America? Or will you, just as a matter of business shrewdness, study what has been done in the past in Greece and Rome, in Egypt and Turkey and India? The business man and the scientist always keep a keen eye on the whole world. And the man of letters cannot afford to do less. If you run over the list of the world's great stylists, you will find that they were, relatively speaking, linguists. I use the term *relatively speaking* advisedly; because in some countries and at certain epochs, a man who knew one language besides his own passed as a person of learning; while in another, two or three extra tongues carried slight distinction. One of our professional humourists once said that he knew a man who spoke seventeen languages, and never said anything of importance in any of them. There is a point at which the brain becomes merely acquisitive. But the possession of two or three languages besides one's own is the best of all aids to a distinctive style. It was James Russell Lowell who said: "The practice of translation, by making us deliberate in the choice of the best equivalent of the foreign word in our own language, has likewise the advantage of continually schooling us in one of the main elements of a good style—precision; and precision of thought is not only exemplified by precision of language, but is largely dependent on the habit of it."

There are, besides, certain advantages to be gained from seeing the purely technical difficulties of language managed with masterly skill in a different medium from our own. We may struggle for years to acquire facility in avoiding harsh combinations of final and initial letters, the exasperating recurrence of some cacophonous but necessary relative pronoun, the jerk and jolt of an awkward rhythm—and at the end of that time we shall not know as much of the philosophy of a fluent and melodious style as could have been learned by one quarter of the effort through examining what can be done in a naturally musical language like Greek; a language in which harsh final mutes have no existence and in which one difficulty of a good prose style was not that of interweaving poetic rhythms, but rather of avoiding them. And similarly we can learn to correct our own tendencies to carry certain principles of prose writing to excess by seeing these same principles carried to a *reductio ad absurdum*. A good illustration of this point is contained in Zola's account of Turgeneff's amazement as he listened to a discussion between Flaubert and his friends regarding that very point already referred to, the pursuit of the one inevitable word:

> Turgeneff opened enormous eyes. He evidently did not understand; he declared that no writer, in any language, had ever refined his style to such an extent. At home, in Russia, nothing of the kind existed. From that day forth, every time that he heard us cursing the who's and the which's, I often saw him smile; and he said that we were quite wrong not to make a franker use of our language, which is one of the clearest and simplest there are. I am of his opinion, I have always been struck with the justice of his judgment; it is perhaps because, being a stranger, he sees us from the necessary distance and detachment.

But whether you accept Turgeneff's view and choose to cultivate the franker use of language; or on the other hand are pleased to pursue endlessly the elusive will-o'-the-wisp of perfection, remember always that style ceases to be good the moment that it is cultivated for its own sake and not simply as an integral part of the whole unified structure. They teach a great deal about the importance of onomatopoeia as practised by Homer and Vergil; and I think that a great many young students gather the idea that it is a quality which ought to flaunt itself before the eye and ear so that as one scans certain lines of the *Iliad* or the *Aeneid* one's predominating thought should be: How wonderfully the rhythm and the consonant pattern here suggests the poet's meaning. Now this, of course, is a fallacy, and there is no better way of showing that fallacy than by quoting Daudet's delicious little anecdote:

> I shall never forget the famous: *Quadrupedante putrem sonitu quatit.* . . . It was always cited to us as an example of onomatopoeia, and my teacher had persuaded me that one might mistake it for the gallop of a horse.

One day, wishing to frighten my little sister, who had a great fear of horses, I came up behind her and cried, "*Quadrupedante putrem,*" and so forth. Well, the little thing wasn't frightened!

Onomatopoeia, like everything else pertaining to style, is used properly when it does not obtrude itself, when it helps us to form a mental picture without our being aware by what agency the author has attained his result. Take, for instance, one of the most extreme instances in modern writing of an attempt to fit sound to meaning—the libretti to Wagner's *Ring.* When you read the text quietly by yourself you feel that the whole thing has been overdone; the various tricks of alliteration stick out like so many bristles. But when this same text is applied to the purpose for which it was intended, you notice none of this, because the sound and the meaning blend so perfectly with the rhythm of the music.

And in all elements affecting style this same principle applies. Any ornament which is used solely because it is ornament, solely because the author wishes to use his subject to call attention to his manner rather than make his manner do obeisance to his theme, is vulgar ornament, as offensive to good taste as over-dress in women. In style, as in everything else pertaining to the craftsmanship of writing, learn to practise "that fine art which so artfully all things conceals."

Chapter 8

# The Technique of Translating

There seems to be a widespread and unfortunate belief that there is no such thing as a technique of translating; or that, if there is, it is a negligible matter—something which is unconsciously absorbed along with the power to render into English endorfian sentences after the fashion of "No, I have not the green umbrella of your deaf grandmother, but the big Russian is up a tree." Translation, so the argument seems to run, is an even simpler matter than original work: the latter requires pen, ink and paper, and a certain natural aptitude; translation requires only pen, ink and paper—the foreign author is expected to supply the natural aptitude. Here, on the one hand, is the book to be translated; and here, on the other, is a stout, able-bodied dictionary which can be relied on to give some sort of an equivalent for each of the foreign words. A little patient plodding and industrious thumbing of the pages—and there you are!

Such is the genesis of a good deal of the mediocre translation which in recent years has brought the whole craft into disrepute. The prevailing modern attitude, in this country at least, is well illustrated by a sentence in a popular novel of the present season. The author, wishing to impress upon us his heroine's want of culture and of literary standards, remarks that she will read anything, ranging all the way from works of real worth to ten-cent translations of French novels. It apparently did not occur to that author that a ten-cent translation of a French novel is quite as likely to be a masterpiece as are the great majority of current American novels which will probably never be translated into any sort of foreign edition, ten-cent or otherwise.

Now, as a matter of fact, there is a technique of translating and one which is neither quickly nor easily acquired. Walter Pater's comparison of translating to a copy of a picture made through tracing paper sounds clever but is misleading. Mechanical aid in rendering one language into another is precisely the sort of aid which must be most scrupulously avoided. The mere ability to hold a pencil and copy the strokes line by line does not even make up the alphabet of the craft. You might spend your life putting tracing paper over Raphael's *Madonna della Sedia* without ever getting more than a caricature of the original. It takes a long apprenticeship and a specially developed skill to enable a painter to produce on canvas a really worthy copy of a great master.

And yet a good many beginners in writing persist in believing that there is a market for their amateur translations. They do not seem to realise that for several reasons there is much more hope for their crude original work than for their equally crude distortions of the work of someone else. Early work usually shows a certain amount of proportion between subject and execution. The great majority of short stories that may honestly be called "not half bad" in workmanship are also "not half bad" in theme. But when a beginner attempts to translate one of the world's classics, or even the latest volume of some widely read modern novelist, he is clothing big thoughts in unworthy phrases and his deficiencies of style are doubly glaring by contrast.

Nevertheless, the practice of translating, as the quotation from James Russell Lowell in the preceding chapter pointed out, is one of the best possible means of acquiring style; and if practised merely as an exercise and without any misplaced ambition for publication, it is a training which cannot be too strongly recommended to the apprentice in the craft of writing. The only trouble with Lowell's utterance is that he limits the value of translation to a single element of style, namely, precision. As a matter of fact, it is one of the most valuable aids which we possess to acquiring an appreciation, not merely of a precision of words, but of new rhythms and new possibilities of linguistic effects. A trained translator of sterling authors soon learns that if he hopes to preserve, with a fair amount of fidelity, the distinctive quality of the original author, he must convey over into his own language something of the linguistic harmony and the phrase cadence. The present writer knows from experience how hard a task this is and what hours of labour it sometimes takes to reproduce in English a single paragraph of French or Italian or Spanish, with even an approximate retention of the original sound pattern add the original number of syllables. Of course, it is only now and then in some passage of particular lyric beauty that care like this becomes imperative; but the ordinary hack translator seldom if ever troubles himself at all about such matters. The ambitious craftsman, on the contrary, may well spend many a day and week after this fashion because he will thus learn a surprising amount of sheer linguistic gymnastics. Translation, whether from Greek, Latin, or some modern tongue, is to the literary craftsman like chest weights and Indian clubs to the college athlete: it brings his mental muscles into training.

Now if we want to train ourselves to translate well, the first step is to get fixed clearly in our minds on which of several principles the best kind of translation is based. It was Lowell who after subdividing translation under the two heads of paraphrase and reproduction, went on to say:

> The paraphrase is a plaster-cast of the Grecian Urn; the reproduction, if by a man of genius, such as the late Fitzgerald, is like Keats's Ode which makes the figures move and the leaves tremble again, if not with the old life, with a sorcery which deceives the fancy.

As between literal paraphrase and a certain degree of freedom, Lowell is undoubtedly right in deciding in favour of the second. Common sense, as well as the verdict of literary history, supports the contention that any translation which is to survive must be the work of somebody possessed of a certain individual bigness, somebody who himself has something to say, something original with which to replace that delicate and volatile essence that is inevitably lost in the process of transference. Of all the arts and crafts, translation is most closely akin to acting. The translator, like the actor, must temporarily sink his personality in that of another; he must speak not his own thoughts, but the lines that are set down for him. But every translator, like every actor, has a right to his own conception of his part; he can, so to speak, supply his own gestures, his own stage business. And, if he is an actor devoid of originality, if he has no ideas to supply, no gestures of his own, no power to make his personality tell upon the stage, then at best his must be a sorry performance. Edgar Allan Poe is not the only writer who has formulated the following theory of the best translation; but no one else has expressed it half so well:

> There is one point (never yet, I believe, noticed) which, obviously, should be considered in translation. We should so render the original that *the version should impress the people for whom it is intended just as the original impresses the people for whom it (the original) is intended.*
>
> Now, if we rigorously translate mere local idiosyncrasies of phrase (to say nothing of idioms) we inevitably distort the author's designed impression. We are sure to produce a whimsical, at least, if not always a ludicrous, effect—for novelties, in a case of this kind, are incongruities and oddities. A distinction, of course, should be observed between those peculiarities which appertain to the nation and those which belong to the author himself, for these latter will have a similar effect upon all nations, and should be literally translated. . . .
>
> The phraseology of every nation has a taint of *drollery* about it in the ears of every other nation speaking a different tongue. Now, to convey the true spirit of an author, this taint should be corrected, in translation. We should pride ourselves less upon literality and more upon dexterity at paraphrase. Is it not clear that, by such dexterity, *a translation may be made to convey to a foreigner a juster conception of an original than could the original itself?*

To produce upon an English reader the identical impression produced by any particular original work upon an ancient Greek or Roman, a modern Frenchman or Italian is, of course, an unattainable ideal. The thing at best can be done only approximately. In the case of the *Iliad,* for instance, a certain dominant note felt by every Greek must have been that of intense patriotism, a thrill of pride at the thought of his own nation's achievements—and of course no dexterity of translation could ever duplicate that thrill in the alien Anglo-Saxon reader. But this is no reason for adopting the fallacious theory of translation laid down by Matthew Arnold in his well-known essay *On Translating Homer:*

> No one can tell him (the would-be translator) how Homer affected the Greeks, but there are those who can tell him how Homer affects them. These are scholars, who possess, at the same time with knowledge of Greek, adequate poetical taste and feeling. No translation will seem to them of much worth compared with the original; they alone can say whether the translation produces more or less the same effect upon them as the original. They are the only competent tribunals in this matter; the Greeks are dead; the unlearned Englishman has not the data for judging; and no man can safely confide in his own single judgment of his own work. Let not the translator, then, trust to his notions of what the ancient Greeks would have thought of him; he will lose himself in the vague. Let him not trust to what the ordinary English reader thinks of him; he will be taking the blind for his guide. Let him not trust to his own judgment of his own work; he may be misled by individual caprices. Let him ask how his work affects those who both know Greek and can appreciate poetry; whether to read it gives the Provost of Eton, or Professor Thompson at Cambridge, or Professor Jowett here in Oxford, at all the same feeling which to read the original gives them.

It is difficult to imagine any method of translation better calculated to distort if not destroy the spirit of the original than this advice of Matthew Arnold's. Whatever impression the *Iliad* made upon the ancient Greeks, it is safe to assume that it was as far removed as possible from the impression that it makes today upon the typical middle-aged professor of dead languages, profoundly versed in archaeology and syntax. It is very much as though he were to say to the contemporary translator of Flaubert or Maupassant: "Do not trouble yourself about what the modern Frenchman thinks of these authors; do not trouble yourself about what the modern Englishman is likely to think; put no faith in what you yourself think—but try to imagine that you are translating for the benefit of a small audience of people who know French as well as English, who by long residence have absorbed the customs of the country and who by nature and training have rather more interest in literature than they have in life." Unfortunately for this theory, it is the ordinary English reader who is going to decide what he thinks of a foreign author given to him in translation; he, and no one else, is the man who must be satisfied. And you can satisfy him only by remembering constantly that a translator is an interpreter and guide. It is not enough for him to know exhaustively the meaning of the original, but he must also realise the limitations of his English audience and foresee what portions of a foreign-work will be unintelligible for other reasons than that of a foreign tongue. The translator of the highest type is in a measure an appreciative and indulgent critic whose first aim is to make his audience share his own enthusiasm for his subject, to bring out not merely some one beauty, but all the beauties of the original; to make us feel not merely an author's theme but his individual style, not only the action of his story but its pervading atmosphere.

Let us ask ourselves briefly what are the requirements for this ideal type of translator. He must have, first of all, a thorough mastery of the foreign language, and secondly, of his own; he must have a special and intimate acquaintance with the author he has undertaken to translate, and lastly, he needs an intuitive sense of the limitations of the public for whom he is translating.

Now, when we speak of a thorough mastery of a foreign language, we mean that sort of knowledge which grasps the sense of a printed page without conscious effort, appreciating all those nicer subtleties of language that lie beyond the reach of grammar and lexicon. There are translators who from long practise can glibly roll forth a smooth and readable translation from a book they have never seen before at a speed which taxes the power of their stenographer to keep pace with them. No matter how experienced translators of this sort may be, they are to be mistrusted for work demanding a *fine* linguistic appreciation. There is in all work of a high literary order a certain quality peculiar to the genius of the language. As your eye travels down the printed page you catch something which you know can not be carried over in full measure into another tongue; you must pause and hesitate and reconsider in a constant and ever recurring effort to reduce such sacrifice to a minimum. And for this reason, when you see another translator pushing blithely onward undaunted by such difficulties, the natural conclusion is that he is afflicted with a certain mental color-blindness, serenely unaware that he is missing the more delicate shading of verbal tones.

And the same nicety of sense of the meaning of words, the rhythm and cadence of sentences is demanded of the translator regarding the language into which he is translating. A far greater wealth of resource is needed by him than by the original craftsman. A writer who is doing creative work is free to choose his own vocabulary; he may affect the abruptness and simplicity of Anglo-Saxon monosyllables or he may emulate what Carlyle has called the "fine buckram style" of Dr. Johnson; he may use few words or he may roll them out in a rushing, surging flood. But the translator is in all these respects bound by his foreign model; he, more than any other writer, must be possessed of an infinite resource of word and phrase—because sometimes only a hair's breadth lies between humour and pathos, between the tragic and the grotesque; and that hair's breadth the translator is bound to preserve.

Thirdly, before trying to put into English even some very simple and very brief piece of writing from a foreign pen, it is your duty as a good craftsman to know your author—not merely to know the one specimen of his work that you are translating but a sufficient number of his volumes to give you the right to claim an intimate knowledge of his style, his structure, his philosophy of life. You may be able to produce a fairly adequate rendering of *Une Passion Dans le Desert* or of *La Fete à Coqueville* without ever having heard the phrases, Comedie Humaine or Les Rougon-Macquart. Yet it is safe to say that there would be something missing, something of that intangible personality which lies behind the words and which would persistently elude any translator who was not thoroughly imbued with the writings of Balzac or of Zola in their entirety. I remember a striking instance of this in the case of a translation published some years ago of Stendhal's *Chartreuse de Parme*. Now anyone who is familiar with Stendhal knows that his style was short, abrupt, rather bold, formed as he himself ironically insisted on a daily reading of the Civil Code. But this the translator in question did not happen to know; it was safe to assume that aside from the *Chartreuse de Parme* he had never read a line of Stendhal. And not liking the plainness of the style and quite missing the terse, crisp forcefulness of it, he proceeded to embellish it in the English translation, smoothing and amplifying and incidentally falling into numerous amusing blunders. The simple statement, for instance, that a carriage was heard "approaching at a trot," was expanded by the translator into "the brisk trot of the two sturdy little horses," regardless of the fact that the context showed that the carriage in question was a one-horse vehicle.

And, fourthly, it is essential to keep in mind the limitations of the special public for whom you are translating. A version of a classic author intended as a "crib" for college students is necessarily a very different sort of production from a rendering intended for the general reader. In the former case, the intention is to emphasize the points of difference between classic habits of speech and thought, and our own; in the latter, the intention is to disguise these points of difference. The one translation says: here is an unaccustomed road, steep and craggy and full of ruts; jolt over it as best you can. The whole purpose of the other is to make the road so smooth that you almost forget that the road lies in a foreign country.

The words *almost forget* are used advisedly. We have seen that the aim of the ideal translation is to place us as nearly as possible in the place of readers for whom the original is intended. Now, take a French novel, the scene of which is laid in Paris. A Frenchman, reading this novel, would on the one hand feel no sense of strange environment; but, on the other, he would not for a moment lose sight of the fact that the action was taking place in Paris, and there is but one Paris in the whole wide world. Now, in translating, it is impossible to preserve both these impressions; you must either in a measure sacrifice the environment, the *milieu,* or else you must convey to the Anglo-Saxon reader some sense of strangeness. It is a matter of compromise, and no general rules can be laid down. Take for example, the whole question of street nomenclature; To the reader with no knowledge of a foreign tongue, *rue* and *strasse* and *via* and *calle* necessarily strike the eye and ear with a certain degree of queerness—yet, to call these foreign public ways *streets* would seem still queerer. One expects the signs in a foreign city to look different, just as one expects to be wet when one goes in swimming. It is not the normal rule of life to be wet, but it would seem considerably queerer to go in swimming and remain dry. It was possible for Thackeray, in light verse, to say whimsically, "Rue Neuve des Petits Champs the name is, The New Street of the Little Fields"; but it would be sheer grotesqueness in serious prose to speak of the Place of the Star, and the Avenue of the Elysian Fields.

Similarly, foreign titles of courtesy and conventional terms of address cannot be translated without producing a curious hybrid effect utterly out of tone with the context. *Mme de Montespan* has a foreign sound; *Mrs. De Montespan* is neither more nor less than burlesque. Even the least travelled modern reader knows that in Berlin people greet each other as *Herr* and *Frau,* in Florence as *Signor* and *Signora,* and not as *Mr.* and *Mrs.* Of course there are certain anomalous cases that are rather baffling; in Germany especially the complicated forms of address, *Herr Ober-Lieutenant, Frau Professorin,* and the like, lead the translator between a Scylla of inconsistency and a Charybdis of farce-comedy. Here, as always in translating, the one safe rule is compromise—and in this the instinct of the born translator is revealed.

But there are certain problems, certain pitfalls, that cannot be foreseen, any more than they can be classified, which every now and then arise to disconcert and hamper the translator, usually at a moment when everything seems to be running most smoothly. There are, for instance, certain plays upon words, certain effects dependent upon the sound or cadence of the original that is simply untranslatable. Mr. William Archer, in his preface to the collected works of Ibsen, points out that this type of difficulty is curiously frequent in the writings of the great Norwegian dramatist, and cites in particular the following illustration:

> In not a few cases the difficulties have proved sheer impossibilities. I will cite only one instance. Writing of *The Master Builder,* a very competent, and indeed generous, critic finds

in it "a curious example of perhaps inevitable inadequacy. . . .
'Duty! Duty! Duty!' Hilda once exclaims in a scornful outburst,
'What a short, sharp, stinging word!' The epithets do not seem
specially apt. But in the original she cries out, 'Plight! Plight!
Plight!' And the very word stings and snaps." I submit that in this
criticism there is one superfluous word—to wit, the "perhaps"
which qualifies "inevitable.". . . It might be possible, no doubt, to
adapt Hilda's phrase to the English word and say, "It sounds like
the swish of a whip lash," or something to that effect. But this is
a sort of freedom which, rightly or wrongly, I hold inadmissible.

An analogous case, in my own experience, occurred in an attempt
to translate the opening chapter of *Don Gesualdo,* from the Italian of
Giovanni Verga. It went quite smoothly—Verga's style is the essence
of simplicity—until I reached the place where the Trao Palace is on
fire, and old Don Ferdinando, "looking like a madman, with a face
of parchment, kept repeating asthmatically, precisely like a duck:
'This way! this way!'" Now, in English this statement seems devoid
of significance; it is not the habit of any ducks of which we have
ever had experience to repeat "This way! this way!" It happens,
however, that what Don Ferdinando said in Italian was, "Di qua!
di qua!"—which seems to be fairly good duck language, whether
in Sicily or America—but unfortunately one of those happy effects
that refuse to be translated.

Lastly, a word or two of practical advice about the best way of
achieving results in translating. Remember that the translator is in
a certain sense a dual personality; he must be on the one hand a
born Frenchman, and a born Englishman or American on the other.
Now, no one can be to the full extent these two things at once; and
therefore no flawless piece of translating can be produced at a single
sitting. The best way, then, is to saturate yourself with the foreign
language, and make a first rough draft in English, as complete as
possible, but clumsy in vocabulary and ragged in idiom. Put it away
for a few days; and then, with the original out of sight and out of
mind, proceed to recast and to refine. A good translation is like a
good vintage; the first draft is simply the pressing of the grapes—the
best you can do is to make sure that you have expelled the juice to

the last drop. But you must give it time to age, before it is ready to be put on the market.

www.ingramcontent.com/pod-product-compliance
Lightning Source LLC
Chambersburg PA
CBHW022120280326
41933CB00007B/468